Praise for *The Email Warrior*

"As a big believer in lists, there's one list that I don't like—a long list of emails sitting in my inbox! Everyone dreams of having zero inbox, but it can seem like a daunting and unattainable goal. Not anymore! *The Email Warrior* is the perfect complement for busy professionals who need a succinct, practical guide to help corral an unruly inbox."
—Paula Rizzo, best-selling author of *Listful Thinking: Using Lists to Be More Productive, Highly Successful and Less Stressed*

———

"Ann likes to call us Email Warriors, but I think she's turned us into email magicians. There's something truly magical about not having email rule your life, even if you have to deal with a lot of it."
—Daphne Gray-Grant, The Publication Coach

———

"This book will change how you think about and manage your email on a daily basis. In this eminently practical, insightful and entertaining book, Gomez will walk you through a simple, practical and—best yet—attainable process to maintain a clear inbox."
—Chris Bailey, international best-selling author of *The Productivity Project: Accomplishing More by Managing Your Time, Attention, and Energy*

———

"We brought Ann in to lead an Email Warrior program for lawyers at our firm. They embraced the many valuable lessons. For some, the program was truly a game changer—experiencing the thrill of clearing their inboxes of thousands of messages, being more disciplined on how and when they spent time on email, and even reclaiming more time for 'thinking.' "
—Karen Bell, Senior Director, Professional and Client Education McCarthy Tétrault LLP

D0916296

"I've always seen email as a great tool but also a productivity killer! Until I adopted the Email Warrior approach, I assumed keeping an inbox clear was unachievable. Learning and adopting the approach has revolutionized how I work. Email is so much easier to manage now! It takes less of my time, my colleagues get responses more quickly, and overall, I have less email. Even returning to work after a vacation has become easier. Within a day, I'm able to get my inbox to less than one screen. I am happy to say that I have not looked back since becoming an Email Warrior."

—Dave Jones, insurance industry executive

—

"Our sophisticated clients demand that we work with the utmost efficiency, and becoming an Email Warrior goes a long way to ensuring that this expectation is met. We have encouraged all of our lawyers to become Email Warriors."

—Deborah Glatter, Director, Practice Excellence, Advancement & Career Development Cassels Brock & Blackwell LLP

—

"A practical, insightful and entertaining read. This approach has changed how I work. I wish I had read this book years ago!"

—Laura K. Williams, Principal, Williams HR Law Professional Corporation

—

"Our Legal Team in Montreal used the excellent and very practical Email Warrior approach to deliver real results—less stress about our inbox, more productive, less email, better emails, more real conversations, better relationships, and when things get hectic or after a vacation, we know how to get back to less than ten emails in our inbox. Just awesome!!"

—Suzanne Morin, VP and Associate General Counsel, Québec and Enterprise Chief Privacy Officer, Sun Life Financial

THE EMAIL WARRIOR

HOW TO CLEAR YOUR INBOX
AND KEEP IT THAT WAY

ANN GOMEZ

Published by Saturn Books
An imprint of Clear Concept Inc.
9251 Yonge Street, Suite 8922
Richmond Hill, ON, Canada L4C 9T3
(905) 237-1651
www.clearconceptinc.ca

Layout and cover design: Duncan Watts-Grant,
wattsgrantcreative.com

Cover image: (also pages 13, 41, 63, 113): iStock.com / Zhev
Image of computer (page 18): BigStockPhoto
Author photo: Bogner Photography
Editing and indexing: Naomi Pauls, Paper Trail Publishing

Cataloguing data available from Library and Archives Canada

ISBN: 978-0-9958346-0-6 (paperback)
ISBN: 978-0-9958346-1-3 (e-book)

Printed in Canada by Island Blue Printorium Bookworks

BONUS TRAINING

Ready to clear your inbox and keep it that way?

Watch The Email Warrior companion
video series at no extra charge.

You'll get in-depth training about how
The Email Warrior system works.

Get your videos at:

https://clearconceptinc.ca/bonusvideos/

To my amazing team, who inspire and support me:
Frances, Geraldine, Marisa, Sarah, Susan and Teresa.

And to my best friend and husband, Enrique.

Contents

Introduction / 1

I Email—The Good, the Bad and the Ugly

1   The Good: Our Love Affair with Email / 15
2   The Bad: Email Consumes Our Day / 21
3   The Ugly: Email Is Addictive / 31

II Flawed Strategies—What *Not* to Do

4   Flawed Strategy 1: Multi-tasking / 43
5   Flawed Strategy 2: Triaging / 51
6   Flawed Strategy 3: Hoarding / 57

III Email Warrior Strategies

7   Introducing the 3D Approach / 65
8   Strategy 1: Dedicate Time / 69
9   Strategy 2: Do It / 83
10 Strategy 3: Defer It / 105

IV Becoming an Email Warrior

11 Step 1: Build Your Master Plan / 115
12 Step 2: Streamline Your Storage System / 133
13 Step 3: Clear Your Inbox / 147
14 Take the 30-Day Challenge / 159

Acknowledgements / 167
Notes / 169
Index / 181
About the Author / 184

Introduction

When I first started using email, back in 1995, I was pretty good about clearing out my inbox. After all, I was getting only about 20 emails per week. Then I started to get 20 emails a day and I found it harder to keep up. By 2010 I was getting 20 emails an *hour* and I threw up my hands in surrender.

I remember a time when I absolutely was *not* on top of email. It was 2001 and I was working as a management consultant on large project teams filled with hard-working, detail-oriented and extremely productive people. They were also email junkies. Messages flew back and forth between us all day long and well into the evening. Keeping up with the constant stream was futile, and everyone around me seemed resigned to having an overflowing inbox. We were all convinced that the only realistic way to manage email was to skim across the surface and do our best to watch out for important messages.

Of course, like everyone else, I had key messages slip through the cracks. Information took longer to find. And I always felt as though I was playing a digital catch-up game. My only solace was the knowledge that I was not alone; everyone was operating this way. Except for one person. My friend and colleague Shilpa always seemed to keep her inbox relatively clear. She never seemed to have more than four emails in her inbox at any one time. They say "Seeing is believing," but I still felt a bit of disbelief whenever I had the chance to peer over her shoulder (which happened quite often while we sat side by side crunching data late into the night). After I overcame my envy, I started to become really intrigued about how she managed her email.

Seeing that it was possible to have an empty inbox inspired me to figure out how to accomplish this myself. I started asking people (like Shilpa and many other email pros I encountered) exactly how they were able to keep up with their email. I read everything I could about email management, and I did a fair bit of experimenting myself.

A committed CEO

"I've been an Email Warrior for as long as I've been using email. I learned early on in my career that it wasn't helpful to read any email multiple times. While I occasionally scan for urgency, I am committed to only ever checking an email one time. This one principle has enabled me to keep my inbox relatively clear despite receiving hundreds of emails a day across several different CEO positions in my career."

—Michael Cloutier, Partner, Mirador Global

Although I moved on from that consulting job, the email volume did not decline. In fact, it only went up. I have continued to barrel along the email highway, and thankfully I have learned some helpful tips to keep me on track. I wrote this book to pass along these tips to you.

Your interest in reading this book probably means you are keen to take control of *your* inbox. Perhaps you find email consuming far too much of your day—both at work and at home. You might find email more distracting than it should be or feel overwhelmed by the volume of incoming email. You might also think, as I once did, that maintaining a clear inbox is hopeless and the only solution is to spend *more* time on email—but you don't have any more time to give.

Luckily, there is a better way. Despite how prolific email has become, some of us have figured out how to contain it. My colleagues and I at Clear Concept, a productivity training organization, are dedicated to helping people become more productive. This includes helping them to become proficient email managers. We like to call these people Email Warriors. And you can become an Email Warrior as well.

> "Inbox Zero" was coined by Merlin Mann of 43 Folders to advocate keeping your inbox clear and simplifying your life.[1]

This book will demystify the strategy for maintaining a clear inbox. You are only a few short hours away from a radically different way of working. As an Email Warrior, you will take back the reins of control over your email inbox. Email will no longer overwhelm you. Rather, you will view it as a strategic and beneficial tool. You will spend *less* time on email and you will get more done. The benefits will extend far beyond your inbox.

The most fascinating thing I have discovered while leading clients through this approach is that the way people manage their email has a strong correlation to how they manage their day. Productivity is the sum of many small steps, right down to how one handles a single digital message. The techniques outlined in this book will help you to focus on your priorities, enabling you to become more proactive and better manage your most precious resource—your time.

Why become an Email Warrior?

Keeping your inbox clear may seem like an ordinary thing, and in many ways it is. However, the common things are often the ones that make the biggest impact. And ironically, the common things are not always commonly embraced. You have the power to change that. You have the power to clear your inbox and keep it clear. You have the power to become an Email Warrior.

That said, it does take work to change your email habits. Before you do this work, it helps to consider the many compelling benefits of becoming an Email Warrior. The most obvious benefit you will gain from this book is step-by-step instruction in how to effectively manage your email so it no longer consumes so much of your time and energy. You will also learn many other valuable lessons leading to even greater productivity gains, which will impact many areas of your work and life. You will experience many associated benefits, which include:

- *Clear focus on priorities.* Maintaining a clear inbox shines a spotlight on what you do (and do not) have time to do. You make more efficient decisions, are more strategic about your commitments and focus more on getting the important things done.
- *Fewer missed messages.* The fewer emails you have in your inbox, the less likely important messages will be missed.
- *Less time wasted.* A clogged inbox leads to a lot of time spent repeatedly sorting through the same emails, scanning for outstanding tasks. With a clear inbox, you will spend less time *sorting* and more time *doing.* With email no longer completely consuming you, you'll have more time for top priorities.
- *Better decision-making.* When you are committed to clearing your inbox, you are much less likely to delay a decision. You avoid pondering something that can be decided in the moment. Email Warriors recognize that progress is more important that perfection. Success comes to those with an action-oriented mentality.
- *Greater reliability and consistency.* When you process all of your emails with the goal of clearing your inbox, you are more likely to get back to people in a more consistent or predictable amount of time. Alternatively, non-Email Warriors tend to be more inconsis-

tent. Sometimes they respond within five minutes. Other times they take five weeks.

- *Improved focus.* Email Warriors resist letting low-priority emails remain in their inbox, where the emails serve as a distraction. Instead, they quickly get these emails out of their inbox. This practice will allow you to spend more time on your top priorities, which in turn will make you more effective.

- *A reduced backlog.* When your inbox is cluttered, you tend to have countless unfinished tasks and a big backlog. You find yourself forever scrambling to keep up with deadlines, rushing at the last minute, never able to pause and strategize, and never quite feeling ahead of the game. A clear inbox helps you stay focused on current tasks and manage deadlines. This leads to better-quality work and a greater sense of accomplishment.

> "The secret of success is to do the common things uncommonly well."
> —John D. Rockefeller

- *Less time spent on email overall.* This strategic approach to email management helps you spend *less* time on email and *more* time on other top priorities. But you still remain responsive and accessible as needed.

With so many benefits to being an Email Warrior, you will soon come to view email as a strategic ally rather than a burdensome drain. More importantly, you will start to notice a positive impact in many areas of your career and life. This book is your road map.

How to become an Email Warrior

This book will help you clear your inbox and keep it that way, regardless of whether you currently have 500 or 5,000 or even 50,000 emails in your inbox. You will learn how to streamline your email use and transition away from having email alone dictate your day. You'll end up spending less total time on email, while still providing senders with reasonably prompt (although not instant) responses.

You are literally three hours away from clearing your inbox and adopting a radically different way of operating. To make this book as practical as possible, it is divided into four key parts, as follows.

I. *Email—The Good, the Bad and the Ugly.* Email changed the way we communicate and we fell in love with it. But this love affair soon turned into an addiction that started to consume our thoughts and dictate our day. Email is now one of the biggest addictions we have ever faced. This section highlights why email is so addictive and challenges the need for relentless email use. For more on this topic, see the notes at the end of this book.

II. *Flawed Strategies—What* Not *to Do.* This part introduces the three most common (and flawed) strategies people use to manage their email: multi-tasking, triaging and hoarding. These strategies lead to distractions, redundancy and disorganization. Collectively, these strategies make us less productive and more frustrated.

III. *Email Warrior Strategies.* To counter any flawed strategies you may be using, this section teaches you the most effective way to process email—the 3D Approach. This includes *dedicating* time for email, *doing* the relevant task the first time you touch an email, and understanding when and how to *defer* tasks that cannot be done today.

IV. *Becoming an Email Warrior.* Finally, and most exciting, this part walks you through a simple three-step process to help clear your inbox, regardless of how many emails it currently holds. Like many busy people, you may think clearing your inbox is easier said than done. On the contrary, becoming an Email Warrior is well within your reach.

Once you clear your inbox, you will be encouraged to commit to a 30-day Email Warrior Challenge. You can join

Something truly magical

"I get more than 300 emails a day (excluding spam) and need to respond to most of them. Before becoming an Email Warrior, this meant I spent some days doing almost *nothing* other than dealing with email. It was both painful and totally inefficient. Even worse, however, I frequently cherry-picked—dealing only with those emails I felt like answering and letting the others languish in my inbox.
I couldn't figure out a solution because I assumed the problem was the sheer volume of email I had to deal with. But I was wrong! With the help of Ann's method, I discovered that email is best tackled in batches and I learned to prevent myself from even *opening* email unless I had the time to handle it only once. Ann likes to call us Email Warriors, but I think she's turned us into email magicians. There's something truly magical about not having email rule your life, even if you have to deal with a lot of it."

—Daphne Gray-Grant, The Publication Coach

a community of other Email Warriors determined to find a better way of working. As part of this community, you will learn more email strategies to help keep your inbox clear. You will also gain inspiration from your fellow Email Warriors and establish a long-term habit that will serve you well throughout your career.

As a time-strapped, results-oriented person, you may be tempted to skip right to Part IV. However, I encourage you to invest the short amount of time required to absorb the valuable lessons in Parts I, II and III, which will form an important foundation. Without these key lessons, you can still clear your inbox. But you won't necessarily change your long-term email habits, and you might find emails pile up in your inbox very quickly again. The goal of this book is to help you embrace a long-term change.

Are you ready to begin this journey? I am honoured to be your guide. You are embarking on a path that has the potential to transform how you manage your time. While this may sound lofty, I have seen it happen again and again. When you get better at managing email, you get better at managing your priorities, and then you get better at managing everything that consumes your time. With the will to change, some dedicated time and a plan, before you know it, you will be an Email Warrior. But first, it's useful to take a quick look back, reminding ourselves where we came from and why email came to be so pervasive.

I

Email—The Good, the Bad and the Ugly

1

The Good: Our Love Affair with Email

Email has been a mainstream communication tool since the 1990s. And even though its appearance is relatively recent, it is hard to recall what life was like before email. Apparently, we were still quite productive without it. We used to call each other, discuss things in person and mail physical documents more often. Life moved more slowly, but we still got things done. Without the ease that email affords, we were forced to prioritize our communications and our focus. Email has increased the speed of business, but it has also created tremendous communication and decision-making bottlenecks. Ironically, now email seems to be the reason we *can't* get things done.

But certainly, in the beginning, we had a love affair with email. I remember eagerly anticipating responses while logging in to email back when it was new. Here are some of the reasons why we had such a glorious honeymoon phase with email:

- *Speed of collaboration.* Clearly, email sped up the rate at which we can transfer information, from the comfort of our home base. Messages travel around the world in an instant, with far less travel involved. We no longer need to rely so heavily on paper mail, couriers and those painful inter-office memos. Remember the day when we had to sign our initials as evidence that we had reviewed a document and then pass it along to our colleagues? It took weeks to share information!

- *More communication and transparency.* Email helped to take us from one-to-one communication to one-to-many communication. Sure, we had meetings and conference calls in the past, but we could still only include a select number of people. Now we can email everyone across an organization in an instant. And everyone has a voice, from the senior executive to front-line employees.

- *More documentation and less paper*. Email allows us to document communication in a way we didn't have access to when we relied more heavily on phone calls and reports. Yes, we could summarize conversations in a memo, but this additional step took extra time and was often skipped. Email also allowed us to share this documentation in a digital format, which is easier to organize, store and search through.

Email has grown fast and furiously, and for good reason. Given this, it seems appropriate that we pause to consider where we have come from, where we are, and where we need to go, to ensure we keep using this tool to boost our productivity—rather than having it slow us down.

Where it all started

Predating the Internet, email began as the digital equivalent of leaving a note on someone's desk. It was a way to put a message in another user's directory that they could retrieve upon logging in. Faculty members in the computer science department at the Massachusetts Institute of Technology were doing this back in 1965.[1]

Soon after, the invention of the Internet enabled messages to be sent from one computer to another one outside the organization. Professor Leonard Kleinrock from the University of California, Los Angeles sent the first Internet message to a computer at the Stanford Research Institute on October 29, 1969, at 10:30 p.m. The first message was "LO," which was supposed to be "LOGIN" but was truncated when the system crashed.[2]

Not until two years later were users reliably able to send messages to users on other computers. Ray Tomlinson sent the first networked email in 1971, using protocols that allowed messages to be sent from one computer to another. After much thought, Tomlinson settled upon using the symbol @ to denote sending a message from one computer to another. Email addresses were designed to denote the sender using the protocol user@host.[3] Jon Postel, one early user, described email as a "nice hack."[4] This description hardly predicted the huge impact email would have and its rapid proliferation. Tomlinson worked on email during his free time, merely pursuing it out of interest.[5] He reportedly said to a colleague, "Don't tell anyone! This isn't what we're supposed to be working on."[6]

This cool invention rapidly gained a broad following based on its communication appeal. We could suddenly reach out to people whenever and wherever we wanted to—regardless of whether they were available at the exact time. Asynchronous communication was enabled, and we no longer had to catch people on the phone or between meetings. Yes, we had voicemail and of course letter mail at our disposal, but email suddenly offered an extremely convenient way to transfer information and reach multiple people at once. Email undoubtedly led to a tremendous boost in our productivity.

From duct tape to high-speed

I remember my very first experience with email. During my undergraduate program in the early 1990s, I was work-ing at the student union. One of the more tech-savvy students set up an intranet that effectively allowed us to email one another using telephone wires strung between offices, taped up with duct tape. While this set-up was not aesthetically pretty, it was a thing of beauty to the tech nerds. Sadly, the system faltered more than it worked, and many of us were left wondering why we shouldn't just walk down the hall to ask someone a question. And the fact is, I was able to complete my degree without the help of email.

By 1999, when I was back in school for my master's degree, *everyone* had email. Granted, we were using dial-up connections that made a horrible, high-pitched *urrrrr-eeeehh* sound while we crossed our fingers, hoping for a viable link. (If you know what I am referring to, you are likely shuddering right now. If you don't, count your blessings that you bypassed that phase in the history of email.) The only saving grace at this stage was that both the volume of email and response time expectations were low, a benefit that gave us time to tackle other important work.

Today, we have access to high-speed Internet connections practically everywhere we go. Even airplanes, the coveted email-free sanctuary, are these days often equipped with Internet connectivity. And if we find ourselves in a rare place without an Internet connection, we can tether our laptop to our smartphone. We. Are. Always. Connected. Obviously, this comes with both benefits and drawbacks.

While you read the next chapter, consider whether the amount of time you spend on email justifies the payoff. I'm sure you'll be nodding in agreement as you read about just how much email consumes our day.

2

The Bad: Email Consumes Our Day

Like most busy people, you may find that processing (sending, receiving or filing) email eats up most of your day. People just like you are spending countless hours every day in their inbox. They constantly have their email open while sitting at their computer. They look at email in the elevator, at red lights and while walking down the street. Anytime they get more than a few spare seconds, they feel compelled to check their email.

In the past, email did not consume our day, and we still had time for other work. We used this wonderful communication tool to transmit information in a simple, low-cost and immediate manner. However, what began as a blessing has turned into a curse. As useful as email is, it has become a burden for many.

Is email consuming too much time?

According to research, we spend between 25 and 50 percent of our workweek dealing with email and, in some cases, even more. To put that in practical terms, if you work Monday to Friday, you might not get to other work until some point on Wednesday, after you've dealt with email.[1] To make matters worse, people say that one-third to one-half of all the information they receive by email is not important to getting their job done.[2] This begs the question as to whether we are getting a justified return on all the time we are investing in email.

Most of us would agree the vast amount of time we spend on email is excessive. From corporate lawyers to senior executives, few people need to adopt the "drop everything and respond" approach to email. They are not like emergency room physicians who need to run at the sound of a code blue alert. If urgent emails do arrive, their senders often resort to other means to gain our attention. People will call or text to say, "Did you get my email?"

An overwhelming volume

With email becoming more and more accessible in recent years through the prevalence of mobile devices, email use continues to rise. Nowadays, the volume of email we manage is staggering. A *New York Times* article once compared emails to zombies. You keep knocking them down but they keep coming.[3]

A 2011 global study estimated that the typical corporate email user processes an average of 125 emails per day.[4] Extrapolate this number over the course of a year, and we process more than 30,000 emails annually. I commonly encounter busy professionals dealing with 200 or 300 or even more emails every day, which makes their annual total even more staggering, at 60,000-plus. Office workers are easily writing the equivalent of a novel (or more) via email each year.

> Fact: Office workers are writing the equivalent of a novel (or more) via email each year.

Relentless checking

Many people check email relentlessly. One study found that office workers check email every two minutes, or about 30 times per hour. This adds up to 240 times in an eight-hour day.[5] Another study reported people check their phone every 6.3 minutes, or 150 times per day, with 23 of these times directly related to messages.[6] Yet another study determined that people check email every time there is a brief pause in their day—or every five minutes.[7]

> **Fact: We check email ten times more than we admit to doing.**

Besides checking email frequently, we are reluctant to let emails sit for mere minutes. Shockingly, 70 percent of emails are attended to within six seconds of arriving, according to a 2003 study.[8] Is our work really that urgent that we need to check email this frequently? Given that people are often checking without responding, the answer appears to be no.

In a worrying trend, many people experience "phantom vibrations." The Pew Research Center reports that 67 percent of cell owners find themselves checking their phone for messages, alerts or calls even when they don't notice their phone ringing or vibrating.[9]

We may not even realize we are checking email this often. Researchers discovered that people were checking email ten times more than they admitted. Karen Renaud, a computer scientist from Glasgow University, and Judith Ramsay, a psychologist at the University of Paisley, also in Scotland, surveyed almost 200 workers. They found that approximately one-third claimed to be checking their in-box every 15 minutes, or four times per hour. Yet monitoring software revealed that they were in reality checking email up to 40 times per hour.[10]

Busy people justify squeezing email into all spare moments in their day, just in case there is an urgent one that needs their attention. They read their emails during meetings, while waiting for the elevator and while stopped at red lights. But all of this email use must make us ask whether we are using email in excess. I believe the answer is yes.

We are always connected

Email is percolating into our personal time. An Adobe study found 87 percent of millennials admit to looking at email throughout their evenings and weekends.[11] They never feel as though they can disconnect, just in case something urgent comes in. After all, email never seems to stop. People drag home briefcases full of other work that did not get done during the day, when they were busy dealing with email. However, this often leads to even more messages bouncing back and forth around the clock.

Email is even seeping into our precious sleep time. Many people check email as soon as they wake up and again right before they go to bed.[12] This is especially true for 18- to 29-year-olds, 90 percent of whom apparently sleep beside their smartphones.[13] People argue that their smartphone is their alarm clock, but it is also disrupting their sleep. Half of those who sleep next to their phone say they check it immediately if they wake up during the night.[14] Email appears to have no boundaries.

Alarmingly, email has even crept into our driving time. A 2015 survey found that 70 percent of drivers admit to distracted driving in some form.[15] Another study found that approximately one-third of people admit to checking email or texts while driving,[16] even though the risk of collision goes up by 23 times as compared to driving when not texting.[17] Drivers who take their eyes off the road for more than two seconds double their risk of a crash.[18] Clearly, checking email while behind the wheel is not a safe habit, not to mention illegal in most jurisdictions.

Not even personal hygiene time seems to be sacred anymore. I was shocked to learn that 59 percent of people check email from the bathroom.[19] (Next time you ask to borrow someone else's smartphone, consider where it might have been.) I once had a client admit he was so addicted to email that he would excuse himself from client meetings so he could go to the washroom—to check his email. When I pushed him on this, he agreed it was a bit excessive to leave one client meeting out of fear that he was potentially missing an email from another client. But at the same time, he didn't agree to change this approach.

Email days and email nights

Natasha was a rising star in her organization, pegged to be the next Director of Human Resources. She was proud of her ability to manage all of the things thrown at her, and she worked hard to respond to people in a timely manner. As a result, she often logged in to email in the evenings to give herself a chance to wrap things up by the day's end. This worked for a time—until her colleagues started doing the same. Instead of clearing her inbox during the evening, her emails seemed to be generating more work. She would email someone at 8:15 p.m. and they would get back to her at 8:20 p.m., which just meant she had more emails to respond to. She just couldn't seem to get ahead, no matter how long she spent working in the evenings. Does Natasha's story sound at all familiar to you?

Email makes us stressed

Several studies confirm something you probably already know: email makes us stressed. In one study, 45 percent of email users associated email with a loss of control.[20]

Another study found that email led to telltale signs of stress, including elevated blood pressure, heart rate and levels of cortisol (otherwise known as the stress hormone).[21] Although it may not be possible to eliminate email altogether, this study highlights the importance of aiming for lower email volume as well as avoiding multi-tasking.

Email is a source of stress for two main reasons.[22] First, email extends the amount of work we do, leading to longer hours and perpetuating the concern about falling behind. Second, the more time we spend on email, the more overloaded and stressed we feel. This creates a vicious circle where higher email usage creates a feeling of needing to spend more time on email simply to keep up.

The most stress-inducing emails seem to be those that demand an immediate response and interrupt work. Conversely, emails that arrive in response to completed work have a calming effect.[23] I keep this in mind when sending emails during non-work hours. If I am requesting work from someone, I often set a delivery delay so they receive the message during the next business day. On the other hand, if I am sending a congratulatory or good-news email, I am comfortable sending it at any time, even if outside business hours.

Email has been one of the greatest workplace stressors for several years now. Even a decade ago, one-third of workers were suffering from email stress, based on the previously cited survey of almost two hundred people by a team from Glasgow University and University of Paisley.[24] Women reported feeling more email stress than men, although both genders were affected. Undoubtedly, email stress has gone up over the past ten years as email use has spiked.

> Is it possible that excessive email use is grounded in an addiction instead of a justifiable need?

What's wrong with checking email?

On the surface, there is nothing wrong with checking email. After all, email contains a wealth of important information and is a powerful collaboration tool. Email also enables us to provide timely responses to our clients and colleagues. Checking becomes a problem when we mistake "timely" for "instantaneous," which is not only unnecessary, but also unsustainable.

Is it possible that excessive email use is grounded in an addiction instead of a justifiable need? Just because we can check email, tune in to a webinar and take a call all at the same time, does it mean we should be operating this way? The next chapter will help you consider this question. Once we understand email's addictive power, we are ready to take back control from email, instead of having it control us.

3

The Ugly: Email Is Addictive

A large email volume and the goal of timely responses do not alone justify the vast amount of time and energy consumed by email. In reality, email tends to be addictive, and about half of us are willing to admit to this. In the fourth annual AOL survey on email use, 46 percent of respondents admitted they were addicted to email.[1]

All forms of social media, including email, are well known to be highly addictive. One study found that the temptation to check social media is stronger than the temptation associated with nicotine, alcohol and sex. This is likely driven by the fact that social media is more readily accessible than the other desires and therefore harder to turn down.

Technology in general is known to be highly addictive. Internet addiction, in particular, has been a hot topic over the past few years. *Newsweek* ran a cover story in 2012 titled "Is the Internet Making Us Crazy?"[2] As the Stanford psychologist Kelly McGonigal stated in her book *The Willpower Instinct*, "There are few things ever dreamed of, smoked or injected that have as addictive an effect on our brains as technology."[3] In addition, technology addiction may be negatively affecting the quality of our life. A study published in the journal *Cyberpsychology, Behavior, and Social Networking* in 2014 suggests that the prevalence of Internet addiction is inversely related to quality of life.[4]

> "The internet is Vegas for brains—a place of over-consumption, indulgence and an electric environment that leaves you forgetting the real life. But at some point you have to leave Vegas and sober up..."
> —Chris Munch[5]

The cost of email addiction

Internet addiction (and, I would argue, email addiction) comes at a cost. For one thing, it appears as though Internet connectivity has affected attention spans. The Statistic Brain Research Institute claims than attention spans have decreased by 40 percent since before social networking and mobile phones became popular.[6] In 2000, the average attention span was about twelve seconds, compared to eight seconds in 2015. In comparison, a goldfish is considered to have an attention span of about nine seconds.

Internet addiction also seems to be changing our brains. In Internet addicts, the brain areas responsible for speech, memory, motor control, emotion, and sensory and other information are 10 to 20 percent smaller.[7] The more time one spends online, the more "atrophy" is seen in these areas of the brain. Research in China has found that web addicts have brain changes similar to those hooked on drugs or alcohol.[8] The areas of the brain negatively affected are involved in emotions, decision-making and self-control. There is now a medical term for this condition: Internet Addiction Disorder (IAD). And while it is not listed in the *Diagnostic and Statistical Manual of Mental Disorders*,[9] fifth edition (commonly abbreviated as *DSM-5*), there is talk of including it in future editions.

We are far too human to resist the temptation to check email when we hear the alluring *ping*. Yet we need to be cautious about responding too readily to these cues, and we should question whether this is the best use of our time in that moment. People admit to checking email almost half of the time (43 percent) simply because they have given in to temptation when they really should be doing something else. As *Harvard Business Review* author Tony Schwartz says, "We spend a crazily disproportionate amount of time seeking the next source of instant gratification rather than pursuing the more challenging goals that ultimately deliver more long-term value and greater satisfaction."[10] Wilhelm Hofmann, a professor at the University of Chicago Booth School of Business, refers to this behaviour as a "self-regulation failure."[11] In other words, checking email may be one of the biggest forms of procrastination in the workplace.

What makes email so addictive?

It may be hard to understand how email is so addictive. After all, email is usually associated with work, and work is hardly considered the most tempting vice (although workaholism is a known social problem). As well, email is not a chemical being delivered into our bloodstream. However, there is definitely something alluring about email. It has an irresistible pull, just as gambling and shopping have for some people.

Email is tempting for multiple reasons. Among these, it rewards our seeking tendencies, provides immediate rewards and is triggered by alerts. Read on to learn more about email's addictive properties. While you do, consider the ways that email has its particular hold on you.

Email feeds our desire to seek

Email provides an abundance of information, making it the perfect fuel for our dopamine system. Dopamine is a critical neurotransmitter (brain chemical) that drives many functions. These include "seeking," a function critical to our survival, as it propels us to move through our world and survive. It makes us curious about ideas and motivates us to search for information (as well as food and shelter). Email rewards our seeking by answering compelling questions such as: Who is reaching out to us? What is new? Is it urgent? Is it exciting?

We have evolved to pay attention to the new thing in our environment. This finely tuned sense is what enabled our ancestors from thousands of years ago to be aware of any predators sneaking up on them in the grass. This sense also makes us intrigued by the new email beckoning for our attention. I can absolutely relate to this when combing through email or surfing the Internet. At times I catch myself still searching long after finding the information I sought. Personally, I have to resist the urge to simply read one email after another in a quest to discover new information.

As well, our dopamine system is most powerfully stimulated when the information coming in is so small that it doesn't fully satisfy us. Short emails that don't provide the full context or emails that initiate online conversations propel us to respond so we can seek more complete information.

Email provides (almost) instant rewards

As humans, we have a strong inclination to favour tasks that offer instant gratification. Email can reward us with some exciting information, new opportunities or glowing reviews. Even if this doesn't apply to all emails, we begin to associate email with intermittent rewards. The anticipation of a reward is more of a driver than the actual reward. Brain scan research shows we have more brain activity when we anticipate a reward.[12] So even without knowing what emails are waiting for us, the anticipation of an enticing or time-sensitive message propels us to check.

Emails (and texts) often serve up a near-instant reward when our fellow email addicts get back to us almost immediately. When we are rewarded for our seeking (with a new email), our dopamine system propels us to seek even more.

In turn, this prompts more email exchanges and an endless loop where we cannot stop checking.

Email is triggered by alerts

Dopamine is very responsive to cues, such as new email alerts.[13] The latter (such as the classic *ding* of a bell) send our dopamine system into overdrive. We can be humming along, minding our own business, when an email alert comes out of nowhere. Suddenly, we find ourselves having a similar response to Pavlov's dog, subconsciously drooling at the thought of the new message. Frankly, if I were in your office and I heard your email alert, *I* would probably want to check your email. Don't worry, I'd restrain myself, but I would find it challenging to sit there, wondering what was new in your inbox.

The double check

One client admitted to checking his smartphone every time he heard the email alert. When his computer buzzed a few seconds later, he also checked his email there—even though he knew it was the same message. He laughed despite himself but also admitted this was going to be a tough habit to break.

Email is unpredictable and sometimes urgent

Email triggers our hungry dopamine receptors, which are stimulated by unpredictable events. This can best be explained by comparing checking email to using a casino slot machine. We find it extremely difficult to pull ourselves away when we think we might be just one coin away from hitting the jackpot. So we keep pumping coins into the machine. Likewise, we never know when a juicy or urgent email will arrive, thus continue to check email relentlessly.

Logically, we might think that the best way to reinforce behaviour is to provide consistent rewards. However, science has discovered that an unpredictable routine has a much stronger influence on behaviour. This is referred to as an intermittent reinforcement schedule.[14] Animals trained in this style tend to work harder for their rewards and take longer to change the behaviour once the reward is removed. After all, they can't be sure the rewards have stopped altogether.

In a similar way, we keep checking emails even when a large number of them relate to routine work and non-urgent matters. When we are rewarded with an urgent or exciting email, we face the equivalent of winning the jackpot. We can't predict when these rewards will come, so we continue to check email frequently. We behave just as if we were pumping more coins into the slot machine.

Email feeds our curiosity

By nature, we are curious beings. One of our most basic human needs is to connect with other people. We are intrigued to learn why someone has reached out to us. Our sense of curiosity helps us to manage risks. After all, we want to identify and manage urgent situations right away. However, once we read an email, we become familiar with it. And once something becomes familiar, our enthusiasm to deal with it wanes. This explains why some emails (which we intend to get around to in the short term) sit in our inbox for six months or even six years.

Email has a (seemingly) low cost

As a society, we are well aware of the costs of some other well-known addictions, such as to drugs and alcohol. But on the surface, an email addiction doesn't appear to carry the same baggage. At first glance, "I'll quickly check email" seems quite harmless. To add to this, email does not have an overtly apparent social cost. Checking email during meetings, during social engagements and even around the family dinner table is often considered socially acceptable.

We convince ourselves that checking email is important work, even when it pulls us away from other priorities. We believe we are being responsive to our colleagues, even though instantaneous responses are both excessive and unnecessary in most cases. We tell ourselves that checking our email takes only a little bit of time, even though we pay a big price in terms of being distracted from doing other work.

Where do we go from here?

The evidence is clear. Email is highly addictive, for all the reasons I have outlined. This pull is so powerful that we will check email even when we know we should be working on something more important. Email has therefore become a great procrastination tool.

The next section explores how a large email volume and its addictive properties have translated into some inefficient email habits. Once we have a better understanding of what *not* to do, we will be better prepared to embrace new and improved email habits.

II

Flawed Strategies—
What *Not* to Do

4

Flawed Strategy 1:
Multi-tasking

Receiving email is akin to standing in front of a tennis ball serving machine. The serving machine fires tennis balls with targeted precision from all sorts of angles. Similarly, we have emails coming at us from many different sources: clients, colleagues, vendors, prospects, publications, friends, family, associations, and so on. With this constant barrage of incoming messages, our inbox quickly becomes a digital potpourri, filled with things that other people choose to send. These include meeting invitations, questions, updates and background information. As author Brendon Burchard wisely said: "The inbox is nothing more than a convenient organizing system for other people's agendas."[1]

In a perfect world, we would hit the tennis balls back (and keep up with the emails). However, sometimes it is hard to keep up with them. Emails start to pile up in our inbox despite our best efforts. Our inbox is *not* an organized ranking of all of our priorities. It is not our to-do list and does not effectively capture all of our tasks, deadlines and commitments. Our inbox is simply one of the many ways we receive information and requests. We need to take control of this information and either quickly process it or transition action items into a well-organized and prioritized plan. We do not want to let these messages sit in our inbox. If we allow ourselves to work from a random assortment of messages remaining in our inbox, we will always be scrambling according to others' priorities and timelines.

Busy professionals tend to spend a great deal of time in their inbox each day. Yet I often find people don't have a clear strategy for how to manage their inbox. I tend to see people using several loosely defined approaches. Some people use their inbox as their to-do list. Some people use it to store reference information. Others use their inbox as a filter as they look out for top-priority messages. Unfortunately, none of these approaches work very well. Without a clear inbox strategy, we are more easily distracted, squander time, lose focus and respond to people in inconsistent ways.

This chapter exposes the flaw behind a very common email strategy: multi-tasking. Unfortunately, many people are convinced that multi-tasking is the only solution to staying on top of email. As a result, they overlay email on top of everything else in their day. They

> "The inbox is nothing more than a convenient organizing system for other people's agendas."
> —Brendon Burchard

jump to email as soon as they hear a new email alert, regardless of what else they are doing. They set up a second monitor simply to track email throughout the day. They look at emails during meetings and personal time. They keep their smartphone on them at all times to act as a backup alert system. They shift their attention every few minutes and remain on "email alert" all day long.

Focusing beats multi-tasking

The brutal truth is that multi-tasking does not work. As tempting as it is to think we can do two things at once, in reality we are simply switching focus from one task to another. Try as we might, we cannot process two tasks at the same time. Rather, we sequentially process tasks. Every time we attempt to do two things at once, we pay a big price. Attempting to multi-task makes us work more slowly, leads to lower-quality work and causes us more stress than focusing on one task at a time. Let's look at each of these pitfalls of multi-tasking in more detail.

Multi-tasking is slower

My colleagues and I have led a simple exercise with thousands of people. In this exercise, we compare participants' time to complete a simple task with the time it takes them to complete the same task while rapidly switching back and forth between two actions. In other words, we compare their times when focusing versus when multi-tasking. And we consistently find it takes people 50 to 100 percent longer to complete a task when multi-tasking.[2]

When we attempt to multi-task, we lose time both in transitioning to a new task (e.g., checking email) and in ramping back up on the original task. If we were in the midst of writing, we spend time reviewing the last paragraph and recreating our line of thinking. *What did that last paragraph say? What were we thinking about before the interruption?*

Once we are interrupted, we often think, "Well, now that I've been interrupted, I might as well get a coffee, or go and talk to Fared, or make a phone call." Studies have found that it takes workers anywhere from 16 to 23 minutes to return to the original task once they are thrown off track.[3] Thomas Jackson and colleagues at Loughborough University found it took the average employee 64 seconds to recover from an email interruption and to return to their work at the same work rate at which they left it.[4] This delay quickly adds up to an hour of lost time each day if one is interrupted by 60 emails in a day.

Multi-tasking leads to lower-quality work

Multi-tasking has been shown to result in more mistakes and lower-quality work. Details are more easily missed when we switch our focus back and forth, leading to more errors and oversights. One study found that people compensate for interruptions by working faster.[5] But this strategy also results in lower-quality work. Working faster leads to making more mistakes, missing details and failing to think through issues with enough depth. Would this be acceptable in your work environment?

Multi-tasking is more stressful

Multi-tasking consumes more energy than focusing on a single task. People report they feel more tired, stressed and frazzled when multi-tasking (as compared with focusing). A team led by Gloria Mark, an expert on workplace interruptions, found that after only 20 minutes of inter-rupted performance, people reported significantly higher stress, frustration, workload, effort and pressure.[6]

"The constant monitoring of e-mail actually reduces productivity."
—Karen Renaud

The research is solid: focusing beats multi-tasking. Try as we might, we are far less efficient and effective when we try to process two things at once. When we choose to look at email, we are no longer paying attention in a meeting, focusing on a report or thinking about another project.

Email and interruptions

Email is one of the most prevalent drivers of multi-tasking in the workplace. Although we receive a ton of emails from others, we can hardly put all the blame on them. At a certain point, we need to assume responsibility for the interruptions.

Gloria Mark has also identified that 44 percent of all interruptions are self-imposed.[7] Choosing to check our email while in the middle of another task is a self-imposed interruption. We allow this to happen. Regardless of whether we are stuck, curious or bored, we need to take responsibility for shifting our attention.

Admit it—you feel like checking email right now, don't you? Sadly, so do I. In our defence, email is a particularly tough distraction to manage for two reasons:

- *We may actually* want *to be distracted.* When we are working on challenging or even monotonous tasks, we might be looking for something more enticing to steal us away.
- *Email is often associated with work.* We justify switching gears because we are attending to other work. Unfortunately, the opposite tends to be true. Email often ends up becoming an excuse to procrastinate on our immediate priority.

Researcher Karen Renaud from the University of Glasgow summed up the situation well. "The constant monitoring of e-mail actually reduces productivity." Renaud goes on to say: "There is a need for increased power, control, and awareness on the part of the e-mail recipient to ensure that e-mail remains a tool rather than a tyrant."[8] Clearly, multi-tasking is a flawed email strategy. In the next chapter, you'll learn about another flawed strategy: triaging.

5

Flawed Strategy 2: Triaging

Jennifer was a busy executive at a large investment firm. She had twelve people reporting directly to her, each of whom emailed her frequently throughout the day. She also received countless more emails from clients and other colleagues. Despite being in several meetings each day, Jennifer tried to respond to new messages as quickly as possible. She admitted to watching for and reading emails anytime a new one arrived—on both her phone and her computer. Jennifer didn't feel that doing this disrupted her day, although she did admit to leaving all non-urgent emails to deal with later.

Her team had mixed feelings about her email habits. When they really needed her help, they tended to hear from her almost immediately. But for less pressing items, they were lucky if they heard from her at all. Every night Jennifer found herself sitting in front of her laptop rereading emails she had not had time to get to earlier in the day. But no matter how much extra time she logged in the evening, she simply couldn't get caught up. Exhaustion always won out, and every day ended with more emails in her inbox than she had started with.

Many people can relate to this story. It depicts a frustrating scenario, to say the least. As a result, most people apply a triaging strategy to their inbox. They start their day by opening their inbox and proceed to read every email to see what work awaits them and whether it is a priority. They repeat this approach countless times throughout the day—whenever an email alert beckons them.

They begin to mentally process the emails as they read them, but then close each one before processing it. They tell themselves that they will get back to these messages later in the day. They tell themselves they are simply looking for urgent messages and prioritizing their work. But they inevitably need to come back and read these emails again. What they don't realize is how much time they lose along the way—time that could have been better directed towards their priorities.

A matter of priorities

The word "triage" is often used in hospital emergency rooms and dates back to World War I, when French doctors would prioritize patients requiring medical attention. The verb *trier* is French for "to sort, select or screen." In other words, injured soldiers were sorted to determine medical priority. This was a necessary approach, given the reality of insufficient resources to treat all soldiers immediately. "Triaging" has been adopted by the business community, where people talk about triaging their work to identify their top priorities.

The problem with triaging

Although we certainly need to prioritize our time at work, triaging email is not an effective approach. Triaging email has many drawbacks, among them wasted time, a growing backlog of messages, and missed deadlines. Let's take a brief look at each of these drawbacks in turn.

Wasted time

The biggest problem with triaging is the redundancy it creates. And this redundancy leads to wasted time. On average, it takes 30 seconds to read an email.[1] If you get 60 emails per day, you spend approximately 30 minutes altogether reading them the first time. If you are in the habit of reading all new emails and then coming back to them later to act on them, you will need to read them a second time. This redundancy adds an extra 30 minutes per day. This might not sound like much, but the time quickly adds up: 2½ hours per week, or 10 hours per month (based on a four-week month), or 120 hours per year, as shown in the following table.

Time spent reading (and rereading) 60 daily emails

Initial Read	Hours
Per day	½
Per week	2½
Per month	10
Per year	120
Redundant Read	
Per day	½
Per week	2½
Per month	10
Per year	120

One hundred and twenty hours is a lot of time each year to spend on a redundant task. That equates to about *three weeks of work time* every year that could have been spent doing much better things both at work and at home, where people often catch up on email. Projects. Business development. Connecting with colleagues. Sleeping. Exercising. Reading. Spending time with family. Going out for lunch. Actually taking a lunch. There are countless other things you could be doing with your time, otherwise lost to redundant reading of emails.

To make matters worse, this estimate of redundancy could be even higher. You might read certain emails three or even four times before acting on them. You might get more than 60 emails each day. And you might be triaging emails on the weekend. All of these situations lead to more time dedicated to a redundant activity: rereading email. As in so many other areas of life, little changes can add up to big results. When we stop rereading email, we end up saving an impressive number of hours in the long run.

A growing backlog

Triaging is the number one reason why emails pile up in our inbox. Triaging focuses our attention on the most urgent or pressing messages. All other "nice to do" messages tend to get left for another time. But the last thing we want to do is cherry-pick our higher-priority and urgent emails, because this alleged "free time" we plan to have for the lower-priority messages never seems to come around.

Tomorrow will bring a whole new slew of emails. Day after day, our inbox swells with less critical messages whose senders are still patiently waiting for our response. Very quickly, these emails multiply into stale, uninspiring screens that weigh us down and create the sense that we will never be caught up.

Missed deadlines

Triaging email also leads to deadlines being missed. Emails we intend to circle back to get lost in a sea of other messages. We legitimately meant to get back to a message, but ended up missing it. In turn, missing a message leads to even more emails, when people prompt us once again.

The bottom line is that triaging email is both inefficient and ineffective. You cannot afford to build this passive, zero-outcome approach into your day. From redundancy to digital clutter to missed deadlines, there is no room for triaging in your busy day. One of the biggest drawbacks to triaging is that it leads to hoarding. In the next chapter, you'll learn why hoarding (at least, in your inbox) is a flawed strategy.

6

Flawed Strategy 3: Hoarding

To keep or not to keep? If Shakespeare were alive today, he would most certainly be asking this question of all the emails flooding into his inbox. Although some people clear their inbox every day, others keep practically all their incoming messages there. The trouble is, keeping excess emails in our inbox is the digital equivalent of keeping every piece of paper related to pending projects on our desk. If we did this, we would be drowning in paper—and inundated by distractions. This chapter briefly examines the flawed strategy of hoarding email, especially the reasons why we do it.

Reasons people keep things in their inbox

From one computer to the next, people are using their inbox for a wide variety of purposes, leading to excessively bloated inboxes. People consistently express a justifiable desire to have access to their information. Consequently, they task their inbox with many functions, including those listed below.

> Far too many people are the digital equivalent of hoarders. I regularly see people with 10,000 or more emails in their inbox and once worked with someone who had over 72,000 emails in his inbox. It's amazing his email system didn't succumb to digital overload.

- *Short-term to-do list*: to keep track of short-term tasks
- *Long-term to-do list*: to keep track of all other things they plan to tackle one day and don't want to forget about
- *Pending tasks*: to remind them of work other people are doing for them
- *Digital filing cabinet*: to store reference items or things they might need again in the future
- *Electronic library*: to store blogs and newsletters they want to read

- *Trash can:* to hold items they'll never need again but just didn't take the time to delete

What about you? Why do you leave messages in your in-box? And on a related note, when was the last time you scrolled down to the bottom of your inbox?

With so many people hoarding emails in their inbox, it is clear there are unmet needs at play. Generally, there are four overarching reasons why people keep so many emails in their inbox:

- *A need to remember.* People worry they will forget to complete a task if it is not in their inbox. They have concerns about succumbing to "out of sight, out of mind."
- *Ineffective folder structure.* People find it takes too long to move emails into folders, or they think they won't be able to find the information again once it has been filed away.
- *Too many tasks.* Some people may be overcommitted and feel they have too many tasks they simply must address in the short term.
- *Unfinished business.* When people are stretched thin, they often take care of the most pressing steps in a task and then jump over to another urgent need. Emails related to these unfinished, non-urgent tasks often remain in their inbox, waiting for their free time, which, sad to say, never materializes.

What from the above list resonated with you? Why do you keep emails in your inbox? Consider this before you dive into the next section: why a clogged inbox doesn't work.

Why a clogged email inbox doesn't work

The problem is, just as multi-tasking doesn't work for us (see chapter 4), it doesn't work for our inbox either. People claim they can simply search their inbox if they need to retrieve something. But when we ask our inbox to do too many things, it fails at all of them. Specifically, here are five drawbacks to having an overflowing inbox.

> Fact: The longer an email sits in your inbox, the more likely it is to grow digital roots, making it harder to address.

- *We forget tasks.* People keep things in their inbox to avoid forgetting about them. But in reality, the more messages we have clogging our inbox, the more likely we will forget something. Thus, hoarding is actually a self-defeating strategy. We lose credibility by not following through on commitments, we create bottlenecks for other people, and we miss out on potential opportunities.

- *We waste time.* When we have multiple screens of email, we are constantly scrolling back and forth to scan old messages to make sure nothing is slipping. This digital equivalent of paper shuffling leads to much wasted time spent searching for and rereading past emails. We could certainly be more productive if we dedicated this time to getting things done.
- *We are more reactive.* A random collection of emails sitting in our inbox is not prioritized in any way. When our inbox is overflowing, the clutter of lower-priority items overshadows those of higher priority. Inevitably, these lower-priority emails distract us and we waste time that should be spent addressing higher priorities.
- *We lose momentum.* We are most likely to address an email immediately after receiving it. Generally, the longer an email sits in our inbox, the more likely it is to grow digital roots, making it harder to address. Think about those emails you have held onto from two years ago. Are you truly going to get around to acting on them?
- *We feel overwhelmed.* An overflowing inbox sends a fairly disheartening message to us about how far behind we are. It is hard to feel in control with countless emails vying for our attention. When our inbox is constantly full, we never reap the satisfaction of feeling up to date.

With all of these drawbacks, hoarding emails in our inbox is obviously not the best approach. We need to get away from thinking about our inbox as our to-do list. Compare your physical office to your inbox. You wouldn't keep all of your work on your physical desk at the same time—or you wouldn't have any room to work! You would also be distracted by all the different papers and have trouble locating the key papers to complete any one task. So you move papers off your desk. The same thinking applies to your email inbox.

Our inbox needs to specialize, not serve multiple functions. It works best with a single, focused purpose—which is to drive action. Let's now consider how we make this happen, through a simple method called the 3D Approach.

III

Email Warrior Strategies

7

Introducing the 3D Approach

Email Warriors know their inbox has one purpose, which is to prompt action. They respond to people in a timely fashion, keep their inbox clear, and manage the time they spend on email so they can focus on other top priorities. You are about to learn how to do the same.

This part of the book will show you how to process your email using the 3D Approach. This stands for three separate actions: (1) Dedicate time, (2) Do it, or (3) Defer it. Here's a quick overview of these tasks, which are discussed in greater depth in the next three chapters.

- *Dedicate time.* Email Warriors dedicate specific time to process their email. They do not try to overlay email on top of everything else they do. They recognize that processing email is a proactive, action-oriented activity. It requires dedicated time and energy to make decisions and take action.
- *Do it.* Email Warriors take action right away, whenever possible, using the One-Touch Principle. They don't simply read an email and then close it to come back to it later. They process it the first time they read it. Their goal is to act. Skipping over an email, waffling on a decision, and only acting on the emails they feel like dealing with, although all understandable behaviours, are not part of Email Warriors' approach to email.
- *Defer it.* Not all emails can be processed immediately, due to a lack of information or a lack of time. Other emails simply cannot be addressed due to other pressing priorities. Still others require us to make a difficult decision or reflect on our options. We might need to "sleep on it." Indeed, some emails need to be deferred.

  The key with deferred emails is to avoid having them clog our inbox. Email Warriors use a Master Plan to record an action item and then move the associated email out of their inbox. They have a streamlined storage system, making it easy to retrieve emails they still need to act on.

The following three chapters will help you master the Email Warrior 3D Approach to email management. Once you do this, you will find it much easier to keep your inbox current. You will no longer simply take a casual stroll through your inbox. Rather, you will view your inbox as a trigger to prompt action. Email will become a strategic ally instead of a dreaded burden.

The 3D Approach to Email Management

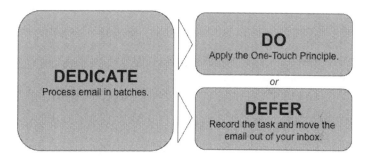

DEDICATE
Process email in batches.

DO
Apply the One-Touch Principle.

or

DEFER
Record the task and move the email out of your inbox.

8

Strategy 1: Dedicate Time

Although email is an important form of communication, our inbox alone should not consume our day. We have other work that warrants our focused attention throughout the day. As we used to say in the consulting world, "Our job is to think." In other words, we need uninterrupted time to concentrate on challenging issues. This cannot happen when we are skimming along the surface and constantly checking email. Dedicating specific times to process our email helps to protect other time for high-quality, in-depth strategic thinking.

Email Warriors only process email at certain times in their day—and they process it in batches. They do not check email constantly. This strategy allows them time to focus on other tasks or people. Email Warriors know that focusing is much more efficient than multi-tasking (and checking email every few minutes is the most prevalent form of multi-tasking in the workplace). In the times they have set aside for email, they process several messages, because acting on ten emails in a row is more efficient than acting on ten emails throughout the hour. Batch-processing is how computers run in an effort to most efficiently use resources. The same strategy works for us, both at work and at home. Consider meal prep. If you make enough meals for a week and put them in the freezer, then cooking dinner each night becomes a breeze (although I admit that I am not speaking from experience on this cooking tip). Regardless, when we batch-process related tasks, we consume less energy in ramping up and transitioning.

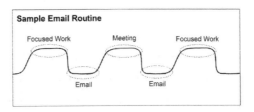

Sample Email Routine

Focused Work   Meeting   Focused Work

Email   Email

Protect time to process email effectively

We have countless things we are trying to fit into our day, from meetings to projects to phone calls to conversations. People often assume they will find a way to tackle email in between all of these responsibilities. This strategy might have worked long ago, when we received only a handful of emails each day. But it rarely works today, given the volume of email we receive.

> If you don't protect the time, you will never have the time.

We absolutely do need to protect time to process email. If we are always trying to process emails on the run, we will not have time to act on the emails. We will always be on borrowed time and won't have time for anything *but* reading when it comes to email. If you are interrupted from one task to read an email, you are likely to read it and not act on it, as you are eager (or feel obliged) to return to the first task. This almost always leads to rework (and redundant reading—see page 54) later on. A more productive strategy is to focus on one task at a time, which applies also to time spent processing email. The key is to commit to either focusing on email or doing another task. People run into trouble when they try to overlay email on top of everything else they do, all day long. You are better off reading and processing two emails than reading ten emails but acting on none of them.

Email is not an urgent tool

To revisit a topic also discussed in chapter 2, unfortunately, email has morphed into a "drop everything and respond" form of communication in many workplaces. Email has come to be associated with a false sense of urgency. With that said, instantaneous email responses are simply not necessary. Unless you are working in the equivalent of a call centre, you do not need to be checking email every five minutes. Most people admit that responses within the hour are more than appropriate (with longer timelines acceptable outside of business hours). If you dispute this, ask your clients and colleagues about their expectations. Even if they expect responses in less than an hour (which will be rare), you still do not need to check email constantly.

If you are struggling to justify a batch-processing approach, remind yourself that email was not designed to prompt instantaneous responses. While meetings and telephone calls rely on people being available at the exact same time, email enables asynchronous communication. One person can send a message at their convenience. The receiver can then respond at their convenience. Email has and continues to work best as a tool that affords us the time to finish what we are doing before diverting our attention to other people's timelines.

What about truly urgent emails?

Some people worry they are going to miss a legitimately urgent email if they are not constantly checking their inbox. Others worry that people will feel they are unresponsive or even rude if they ignore email for any stretch of time. Let's take a closer look at the first issue, which is a common concern.

Suppose your top client sends you an urgent email, just after you turn your attention away from email. You don't even know their message is sitting in your inbox. After all, you are happily focusing on another piece of work. Five minutes go by. Then seven minutes. Then ten. You are completely oblivious to the fact that your client is anxiously awaiting your response. What will happen next? If your client's concern is truly urgent, they will likely call you. And if they can't get through to you, they will call one of your colleagues. They will pursue various avenues until they get the help they need. At the same time, they will hardly fault you for a response delay of mere minutes. After all, some people spend more time in the washroom! More likely, they will assume you are attending to other important maters. For example, you could be in back-to-back meetings with no chance to check email.

The bottom line is even so-called urgent emails can sit in your inbox for a short time. There are other ways people can get in touch with you (such as calling or texting) if someone desperately needs your attention.

How often should you check email?

Your ideal email frequency and duration depends on two things. The first is your individual working style and the second is your work environment. I like to call these the "You" and "Them" factors.

- *The "You" factor.* What is your ideal length of time to focus on one task? How long do you need to truly dig into your work? At what point does your mind start to wander and you crave a transition? How strong is your focus muscle?

  Some people find they can focus for only 15 minutes at a time. Others can stretch this to 45, 60 or even 90 minutes. They intersperse these periods of focused work with a variety of things, like email, phone calls, getting up to talk to someone or taking a break. Research shows that we seem to be able to focus for a maximum of 90 to 120 minutes.[1] We can carry on beyond this time span, but we will not be working at our peak productivity. After this time, we are better off to take a break (to process email or do some other activity) and then resume focus later.

If you find you cannot focus for very long, it's possible you may have lost some of this skill. With the advent of "always connected" technology, focusing is a common challenge. Luckily you can build up your ability to focus with practice. Start with small spans of time and build up from there.

- *The "Them" factor.* The other factor that dictates your ideal email checking frequency is your environment. "Them" refers to your colleagues, clients, friends and family. In essence, this factor comes down to "How long can they live without you?" Obviously, the answer varies based on industry and roles. What response time do they expect? Some people only process email at the beginning or end of their day, with the main part of their day dedicated to meetings. Other people need to process email every hour, given the nature of their job. Regardless, you need to determine how long others can wait for you. Even if this expectation is as short as 20 minutes, you can still dedicate discrete blocks of time to email in between other focused stretches of work. You do not need to be interrupted each time a single email arrives

Admittedly, some workplaces set unrealistic expectations. People you work with might expect responses within minutes. They might expect you to take your phone with you everywhere—from meetings to lunch to the washroom to bed. This expectation is based on the false belief that everything demands immediate attention. In reality, the opposite is true in almost every situation.

After considering both the "You" and "Them" factors, defining your ideal email processing frequency is all about striking the right balance between focused work time and accessibility. These are not competing goals. You can still be responsive while protecting blocks of time for independent, focused work.

How to dedicate time for email

As discussed in chapter 3, email is extremely enticing. Its very nature, including its addictive qualities, makes email hard to process in batches. That said, a number of actions make it easier to adopt a batch-processing approach and manage our email addiction without having to rely too heavily on our own, all too fallible willpower. Among other techniques, you can disable email alerts, turn off your email and park your smartphone.

- *Disable email alerts.* By now, you can probably guess what I suggest you do with distracting email alerts. Turn them off. This includes all bells, lights, icons and pop-up windows. The advice applies to your computer, smartphone, tablet, watch and anything else that alerts you to incoming messages.

Some people convince themselves the small pop-up box with a sneak preview of the email doesn't distract them. They claim this gives them the comfort of knowing an urgent request is not sitting and waiting for them. The problem is, even neutral emails distract us. If you see a simple "Can you talk?" email, you will probably find it hard to resume focus on your task at hand. You'll likely be distracted, wondering what the sender wants to talk about.

Commit to living without the alerts for one week. Then watch how much easier it becomes to focus on other work. Once you notice an increased ability to focus on non-email tasks, I'm confident you'll be more inclined to keep the alerts turned off. Turning off email alerts puts *you* back in control when it comes to email. Now you get to choose how often you check email. You shift away from reactive mode and back into proactive mode.

- *Close your email program.* Turning off email alerts is useless if your inbox is staring you in the face all day. You need to remove the visual distraction as well. Otherwise, you will be tempted to read the unread messages piling up in your peripheral vision.

Close (or at least minimize) your email program when you are focusing on another task. Personally, I find it most effective to turn it off. Simply minimizing my email program makes it too easy to succumb to temptation and jump over to email for a quick peek.

- *Park your smartphone.* More and more often, people are checking email on hand-held devices, which they have access to at all times. Wherever possible, strive to process email on your computer, where you have easier access to your storage system and a full keyboard. Decide how often you will check email on your smartphone outside of working hours and monitor your habits. Resist checking any more often than this simply out of habit.

At the extreme, some people sleep beside their smartphone and wake up in response to email or text alerts. But just because someone emails you at 3:00 a.m. does not mean you need to wake up and respond to the message. In reality, people would much rather receive a response from us when we are rested and clear-headed. If you are using an alarm on your smartphone to wake yourself up in the morning, I recommend you get yourself an alarm clock and park your smartphone in the kitchen. This will remove distractions, along with the temptation to check, and allow you to get your proper rest.

- *Train people how to work with you.* If you are hesitant to batch-process your email, perhaps this is because you have trained people to expect immediate responses. When people know they can reach you anytime, over time they will default to giving you less and less notice. They will not hesitate to send you an email a couple of minutes before the big meeting instead of planning ahead. Their emergencies become your emergencies, for haven't you always been accessible before?

  If you have trained people how to work with you (even unconsciously), you can retrain them as well. Let people know how often you check email (for example, once an hour or three times a day). This information helps them to manage their expectations about your response times. If necessary, you can justify this strategy by letting others know this approach allows you to provide higher-quality work and more thoughtful responses.

  In my work, I strive to check email three times a day. However, if I am leading a training session, I may only check email one time that day. I let people know that I try to respond within the day and ask them to call me (or one of my colleagues) if they need a faster response.

- *Start small.* As you work towards batch-processing email at select intervals, consider starting with small steps. If people you work with are used to immediate responses, you might want to extend that turnaround time gradually. For example, transition from checking email every 15 minutes to every 30 minutes and then every 45 minutes. Gradually extend this timeline (i.e., over several days) until you reach your ideal email frequency. And I doubt you will receive any complaints about your response time in the interim. I would be surprised if your colleagues or clients even noticed.
- *Treat email as a reward.* With or without email alerts, we can be pretty sure emails are piling up when we are focused on other things. Most of us are extremely tempted to see which emails have arrived since we last checked. We might claim to be scanning for urgent messages, but more than likely we are simply feeding our curiosity. We can use this pattern of behaviour to our advantage by rewarding ourselves with an email break after completing something else. I am convinced that checking email is one of the most effective (albeit not the most sexy) rewards in the workplace.
- *Limit your email time.* The actual amount of time you spend on email is highly dependent on your role. If you receive approximately 100 emails per day, you

likely need about two hours to process them. Obviously, this estimate varies based on the complexity of each message. Regardless, protect slightly less time than you think you need for email. Short email windows will encourage you to write shorter responses, make more efficient decisions and resist saying yes to too many requests.

- *Do unto yourself as you would unto others.* We deserve to give our work the same respect we give to others. When we are meeting with one person, we are probably not scanning our inbox for emails from others. At least I *hope* you are giving the other person the respect of your undivided attention. When we are meeting with other people, email simply has to wait. Yet we indulge multiple email interruptions when we are working on our own tasks. We owe it to ourselves to give our work the same level of dedicated attention we give to others.

- *Don't worry about forgetting.* Some people are concerned that they will forget to check email if they turn off their alerts and close their email program. In my experience, this is rarely the case. If you are reading this book, I am guessing there is a much higher risk of your day becoming overwhelmed by email. Forgetting about email—as unlikely as this is—could actually be a blessing in terms of found time.

Overall, there are several things we can do to protect time for email (while not letting email consume our day). Once we have dedicated time for email, it is much easier to process it in the most efficient way. In the next chapter, you'll learn the best way to approach the second *D* in the 3D Approach. This begins with the amazing time saver the One-Touch Principle.

9

Strategy 2: Do It

I remember standing at my father's desk as a young girl as he was processing some of the family bills. He would systematically open an envelope, review the enclosed bill, write a cheque and place it into the return envelope. Then he moved on to the next bill. He collected the bills that came in the mail and sat down to complete this little ritual every week.

I vividly recall him telling me he only ever touched a bill one time. And just like that, my patient father opened my eyes to the wonders of efficiency at the age of ten. Fast-forward a few years (okay, decades), and my dad's advice still rings true. Although I may have transitioned to online bill payments, this lesson has stuck with me. The One-Touch Principle is just as relevant in today's digital world as it has been in the paper world.

> The One-Touch Principle: If something takes less than five minutes, do it now. If something takes longer than five minutes, do it now or identify a time to do it.

Just like my dad with his household bills, Email Warriors strive to act on emails the first time they touch them. They apply the One-Touch Principle to every email. Quite simply, this means processing each email the first time you read it. Don't read it and then close it, assuming you will have time to come back to it later. You'll be too busy tomorrow dealing with a new batch of email. Even if you are able to find the time to come back to it, you are building redundancy into your day.

The One-Touch Principle has the power to completely transform how you process email and also how you manage many other systems in your life.

Clear it out

Once you have acted on an email, you need to clear it out of your inbox. The One-Touch Principle is not completed until the email leaves your inbox. *I cannot reinforce this enough.* The goal of an Email Warrior is to keep their inbox clear. Avoid waiting until the end of the day to clear out processed emails. Instead, do this as you go through your mail; push to clear your inbox whenever you process email.

Emails are not meant to live in your inbox. These messages are in a nomadic state until you process them and move them to their rightful home. Think of your inbox as being like an airport lounge where people sit waiting to board a plane. Your inbox is where messages, like passengers in transit, line up, pending action.

It is up to you to ensure these messages do not stagnate in your inbox. Email Warriors leverage the "Move them out and move on" strategy. After having completed the necessary action prompted by the email, they file, archive or delete the message. Email Warriors do this *before* moving on to the next email. They treat it as a challenge to clear messages out of their inbox as they process them during specific intervals throughout their day. By doing this instead of waiting until the end of the day or the end of the week to clear out messages that have already been processed, they also avoid wasting precious time.

When to use the One-Touch Principle

Obviously, the One-Touch Principle applies to urgent emails. You want to act on time-sensitive emails as soon as you read them. But many other types of information also benefit from the One-Touch Principle. These include emails you need to respond to, information you need to absorb, action items you want to forward or delegate, invitations to meetings, and reference information you need to file. Even if the action is as simple as deleting an email, aim to apply the One-Touch Principle.[1]

Stepping outside of the digital world, the One-Touch Principle has multiple applications. Aim to listen to a voicemail no more than once, put things where they belong, file papers (instead of piling them) and follow up on verbal requests right away, when possible. It is truly remarkable how much time this principle can save.

Short tasks versus long tasks

The One-Touch Principle refers to all tasks—both short and long. If a task takes less than five minutes to complete, you should do it now. However, the actual length of time is arbitrary—if you can do the task now, you should.

Granted, some tasks we simply do not have time to tackle right now. In some cases, we may need to collect more information before responding. Or we may need to reflect on a decision. We can generally tell which emails require deliberation upon first glance.

Email Warriors don't read these emails until they have time to process them. They might do a quick scan of the message and possibly even send a quick reply (for example, "I'll get back to you tomorrow"). But they resist fully focusing on an email until they are prepared to act on it. They only ever read an email one time. There's no need to fully read an email once you realize you cannot process it right away. Protect your precious time and close the email as soon as you realize that you can't apply the One-Touch Principle. Admittedly, this is tough to do. It's very tempting to read the entire email. But remind yourself that any time spent reading will have to be respent later.

Why one touch is better than triaging

Applying the One-Touch Principle has several benefits. As you can guess by now, when you apply the One-Touch Principle to email, you'll save time, reduce your backlog, and lose fewer things. You'll also be a better communicator, gain a work buffer, make more timely decisions and be more consistently responsive.

- *You save time.* The One-Touch Principle saves you time by eliminating redundant activities. As you saw earlier, simply avoiding rereading email easily frees up 120 hours or more per year.

- *You contain your backlog.* The One-Touch Principle helps you keep up with the flow of email and avoid a growing backlog of messages in your inbox. Having a clear inbox makes work (and life) much easier to manage.
- *You lose fewer things.* The One-Touch Principle reduces the risk, inconvenience and embarrassment associated with key messages getting lost (or forgotten about) in an overflowing inbox.

Learning what's possible

As a healthcare executive, Manuel was inundated with email every day. For many years, he assumed keeping his inbox clear was an unachievable goal. But after he learned the One-Touch Principle, he changed his ways. In all but the busiest of days, he was able to get his inbox back down to under a screen. Manuel reflected back on the days when he used to complain about email overload. But he now knows that he wasted a lot of time rereading emails without acting on them. Once he adopted the One-Touch Principle, he never looked back.

- *You communicate better.* When you deal with emails promptly and with one touch, you will be viewed as being easy to work with. Other people will appreciate your consistent turnaround times and the fact that you are not the cause of a delay or bottleneck in their own work.
- *You build in a buffer.* When you don't have an email backlog, you have some buffer for the inevitable unknowns that demand our attention. If, during busy work periods, you are also catching up on older emails or tasks, work becomes that much harder to manage. The One-Touch Principle prevents you from filling up your future time with emails you could deal with today.
- *You make more timely decisions.* The One-Touch Principle encourages you to make efficient decisions. Instead of leaving messages in your inbox, go with your gut instinct and make a decision. As Malcolm Gladwell pointed out in his book *Blink*, our instinct is usually a fairly powerful indicator of the right deci-sion.[2] If you need to ponder whether or not to attend a meeting, your gut is probably telling you that you shouldn't.
- *You take advantage of fresh background and context.* The first time you read an email, you start to mentally process it and consider your response. If you move on

to another task at this point, you will need to recreate all of this thinking later. By contrast, you save time and effort when you capture your initial ideas right away—even if you are only able to answer part of the question in a draft.

Clearly, the One-Touch Principle has the power to fundamentally change how you process email. In the next section, you'll learn how to fully embrace this habit, thus enabling you to take advantage of all these benefits.

How to make the One-Touch Principle work

In theory, the One-Touch Principle makes perfect sense. As we saw above, it saves us a ton of time and also prevents work from piling up. But this principle can be tough to apply consistently. Curiosity often prompts us to simply read (rather than act on) incoming messages when we should be doing something else. And of course, many other important things are vying for our attention and preventing us from acting on emails the first time we read them. Sometimes the One-Touch Principle is easier to think about than it is to apply to our email. To help you out, here are nine concrete ways to make applying the One-Touch Principle more attainable.

1. Process emails sequentially

Imagine you have just landed after a long and tiring flight. You need to go through customs before collecting your bags and heading home to bed. Instead of arriving to find a well-organized lineup, you come to a large room filled with people milling around, waiting for their turn to be processed. There does not seem to be any logic to when people are being processed. The first ones to arrive are not being given priority and called up first. In fact, it seems the people who arrived after you have a better chance of being called up than the people who arrived before you. Soon you get the feeling that the longer you wait, the less chance you have of being processed.

Unfortunately, this scenario reflects what happens to email in most people's inboxes. When checking their email, many people randomly pick which emails they will process. They tend not to go through them in a sequential fashion, but rather in a fairly haphazard and inconsistent way. The longer an email sits in their inbox, the greater the chance that it will languish there. Newer emails always seem to garner more attention.

Processing a lineup of people (or email) sequentially is a much more efficient approach. Theoretically, we need to act upon every email we receive (even if that action is as simple as deleting the message). The best approach is to systematically work through our inbox, treating our inbox like a lineup of messages to be addressed. As a general rule, try to avoid fast-tracking messages based on their level of importance or excitement.

There is some debate about whether we should take a LIFO (last in, first out) or FIFO (first in, first out) approach to clearing our inbox. Email Warriors take a FIFO approach and strive to address the older, staler emails before the fresh, new ones. After all, it seems appropriate that the senders who have been waiting the longest for a response should have their messages processed first. This approach avoids letting forgotten emails stagnate at the bottom of our inbox.

Without a doubt, the more enticing or intriguing emails are at the top of our inbox. Curiosity compels us to look at these first, rather than the older, predictable messages we may have already read. As suggested in the previous chapter, try to use the allure associated with these newer emails to your advantage. Use them as a reward for getting through your older emails.

Sequential processing does not allow for procrastination. When we come across a less-than-ideal task, we dig in and tackle it because it is the next one on the list. Every time we face a decision point in our day, we are more likely to procrastinate. Sequential processing eliminates the decision of which email to tackle next.

Some people argue they will miss updated conversation threads if they start by processing email at the bottom of their inbox. This is a valid point if your inbox contains hundreds or even thousands of emails. But once you are an Email Warrior, and you have only a handful of emails in your inbox, you can likely quickly scan those messages to make sure you are tackling the most recent email in a chain.

> "I will scan my inbox for urgency, but I will only ever read an email one time."
> —Michael Cloutier, Partner, Mirador Global

Agreed, we don't always have the time to address emails at the bottom of our inbox. But we should at least scan them with the intent of processing them during each discrete email session. If we don't do this, they soon get forgotten and lead to clutter in our inbox.

Admittedly, there are two small exceptions to the sequential processing principle: urgent messages and related messages. Read on to find out how to manage these.

2. Scan for urgency

You may be expecting an urgent email that you want to attend to right away. If so, give yourself permission to do a quick "scan for urgency" of your inbox before sequentially processing your email. Sometimes this is all we need to have the comfort to work through our emails in order. After all, we've ruled out any potential emergencies.

This quick scan works as long as it is truly only a quick glance at the senders' names and the subject lines. Doing this adds hardly any extra time to your day. Just make sure not to open and read every single email during this step. Otherwise, you are violating the One-Touch Principle.

You also want to make sure you are only fast-tracking the really urgent emails. Try not to fast-track a message merely because it looks more interesting than the others. If you do, you are ignoring the sequential processing principle and will soon have a backlog of lower-priority messages clogging your inbox.

The challenge here is that scanning our inbox often incites our curiosity. Before we know it, we are opening emails and reading them. Many people (me included) simply can't resist the temptation. An even better approach is to encourage people to call you with any rare, urgent issues that require your immediate attention. Let people know what your typical email turnaround time is, and avoid falling into the trap of scanning your inbox incessantly.

3. Group related messages

There may be several messages in your inbox related to the same topic. In this case, it is more efficient to process these together. Go to the most recent message to capture the most current discussion thread. Once you have acted on the most recent message, clear out all the related messages. Then go back to sequentially processing other emails, starting from the bottom of your inbox.

4. Focus on making efficient decisions

Often we have all the information we need to process an email. But delays can easily come when we don't focus on making an efficient decision. Letting an email "sit" because we don't feel like answering it flies in the face of the One-Touch Principle.

In the words of Nike, *Just do it*. Make decisions in the present. Delayed decisions equal wasted time. If you feel the need to sleep on a decision, at least get your initial thoughts down in a draft email. Reviewing and modifying this draft tomorrow will be easier than recreating your thoughts from scratch.

While we strive to process email sequentially, there is no rule that says you must process every email. But if you're going to skip it, choose to do that now. It's better to delete an email than let a low-value email remain in your inbox.

5. Process email on your computer

The One-Touch Principle absolutely applies to any hand-held device. It is very tempting to simply read, rather than process, email on a smartphone or tablet. After all, these digital devices make email oh-so-accessible. However, you may find it is easier to apply the One-Touch Principle while working on your computer, where you have easy access to a keyboard, important files, digital folders, and so on.

Your smartphone may be a great "scan for urgency" tool, but resist using it to read all of your emails unless you intend to apply the One-Touch Principle. Anytime I see someone walking and checking their smartphone, I wonder how much they are accomplishing. Productivity is about getting things done rather than constantly being in reactive mode.

Instead of relentlessly checking your hand-held device, consider using time away from your computer for another purpose. Talk to someone; read background material; reflect on an issue; meditate; relax. Many people find they don't have enough time for thinking, and this is a perfect opportunity. Give yourself this time and you'll be more refreshed and focused when you resume working again.

6. Manage emotional reactions

Some emails may trigger an intense emotional response. You might be angry, offended or disappointed and tempted to fire off a response you'll regret later. In situations like this, it is better to pause before sending a response. Of course, you can still partially apply the One-Touch Principle by recording some of your thoughts in a draft message (while giving yourself a chance to refine your message later).

A simple rule can be useful to remember at such times: the 24-hour rule. Our kids play competitive sports and many of our teams promote a "cooling off" period. While it is easy to get caught up in little things (which feel like big things at the time), this rule encourages parents to wait a full day before talking about something that bothers them. No shouting criticisms at the referee during the game. No waiting to lambaste the coach outside the dressing room. No throwing jabs at parents on the other side. Rather, allow some time for your emotions to settle down. Then (and if the issue is still important to you) you can engage in a more constructive conversation.

While 24 hours may be too long to wait to respond to an email, the principle still applies. Give yourself time to deal with an intense emotional reaction before sending your response. If you are questioning whether your response is appropriate, it is probably a good idea to pause and reflect. Timeliness should not override respectful communications.

7. Bring your best

When we are rested, well fed, motivated, and so on, it's much easier to apply the One-Touch Principle. Email Warriors know that setting personal boundaries around adequate time for sleep and fitness activities helps them to thrive at work. It is much harder to adopt the One-Touch Principle if we are tired and unfocused. After all, it is easy (and perhaps fun) to simply read an email, but often extra effort is required to do the work associated. Even a task as straightforward as processing email taps into our energy, so we want to make sure we have a good reserve.

8. Change your language

For many of us, the One-Touch Principle represents a radical shift from how we currently work. Therefore, it's important to make a conscious commitment to shift to this new work style. Instead of saying you are going to "check" your email, declare you are going to "act on" your email.

The phrase "check my email" is like casual window-shopping, as opposed to focused power shopping. During a casual email scroll, you may be telling yourself you are assessing or prioritizing, but there is a good chance you are merely feeding your curiosity. This casual scan is guaranteed to cost you excess time, because you will inevitably have to read these emails again. No doubt there are much better things you could be doing with your time.

9. Pretend someone is watching over your shoulder

A little bit of accountability can go a long way. You might want to pretend that someone is looking over your shoulder and noticing when you are (or aren't) applying the One-Touch Principle. I would be happy to be that hypothetical person. After all, I pretend that every single one of my readers is watching over *my* shoulder. This keeps me accountable and encourages me to use the One-Touch Principle, even when I don't feel like doing so.

Deleting: A unique application of the One-Touch Principle

Although there are justifiable reasons to keep certain emails, there are many other emails we should delete. People tend to keep far more emails under the guise of "future reference" than they ever refer to again.

Not everyone makes the time to delete emails as part of their regular course of business. But then they find they have to do a mass delete due to exceptional circumstances. For example, they might have reached their mailbox limit, or maybe they are transitioning out of a job or work role.

Rather than waiting for this scenario (and its associated pain), it is far easier to delete emails as you process them. It is better to keep up with this task rather than having to catch up. Don't leave emails and expect you will have time to go back to delete them. There will always be more pressing and more interesting things to tackle.

Some people claim it simply takes too long to delete or file an email. I would argue that deleting an email takes a millisecond of your time and does not lead to a significant time deficit. The time drain is more likely related to either a poorly organized folder structure or delayed decision process. See chapter 12 for advice on how to streamline your folders and push yourself to make efficient decisions. Once you discover the pleasure and productivity in having a clear inbox, the benefits of filing emails will far outweigh the small amount of time this task takes.

What to delete?

Just as we wouldn't hang on to every piece of paper or voicemail we receive, we should not hold on to every email. While any individual email absorbs very little digital space (assuming it doesn't have an attachment), collectively emails lead to digital clutter. So, to avoid hoarding, push yourself to delete the following emails:

- *Information you might need in the short term.* Even if you think there is a chance you'll need the information in the short term, you can feel quite confident in deleting such an email. After all, most email systems provide a safety net, because you can retrieve the deleted email in the short term from the deleted or trash folder.[3] To be sure, check the settings in your email system.

- *Information you have read.* Once you have read or scanned (and absorbed) something, you probably will not need to go back to it. Blog posts often fall into this category. If you want to clip a quote or key finding from the article, the time to do it is when you read it. Forcing yourself to go back and read the article again in the future creates redundancy. Instead, add the key information to a file with other similar information. I use Evernote for this purpose, but any note-taking or word processing tool would work.

- *Information you can access elsewhere.* You can delete anything from your email inbox that you can readily access elsewhere (e.g., through your organization's database or on the Internet). Search functionalities are so quick these days that you would likely default to checking these other sources first anyways. For example, if someone emails you the latest YouTube video, there is no need to keep an email including the link. If you want to view the video again, you will be able to find it online with a few key search terms.

- *Meeting invitations.* Some email systems automatically load a scheduled meeting into your calendar and delete it from your inbox once you accept it. Other email systems (e.g., Gmail) leave the meeting request in your inbox. In this case, manually delete these. If for some reason you need to refer to the original email again, you can find it in your deleted folder— at least in the short term.
- *Social conversations.* You would never keep a transcript or recording of a social conversation. It doesn't make sense to do this with email conversations either. Enjoy the email conversation for what it is, then delete it and move on. If you need to, make a note of key information and then delete the email. For example, if someone tells you they are bringing brownies to the potluck, you can make a note and then delete the email.
- *Anything you don't intend to read.* Okay, this one is obvious, but it absolutely warrants mention. You and I both know there are countless emails you'll never look at, and you could delete these (or unsubscribe from receiving them) right away.

In summary, do your best to delete many emails as you process them. Keep (and file) only those emails you definitely need to refer to in the future. These might include key decisions, quotes, instructions, confirmations, electronic receipts, regulatory information, and so on. For more advice on clearing out a large email backlog, see chapter 13.

Remember, your inbox is just a temporary staging area. You want to process as many emails as possible in the short term using the One-Touch Principle. Messages will accumulate in your inbox throughout the day, and your goal is to whittle down that number during each email session. Of course, some emails will fall outside the parameters of the One-Touch Principle, and you'll learn how to manage those in the next chapter. But for the vast majority of emails, challenge yourself to adopt the One-Touch Principle. Once you do this, you'll never view email the same way again.

10

Strategy 3: Defer It

We all have a lot of work on the go. And plenty of work tends to come in via email. Ideally, we could keep up with this volume and avoid having tasks pile up. But the reality is, we don't have time to tackle everything that lands in our inbox. At least we don't have time right now. Some emails need to be deferred until later. However, we do not want to leave these emails in our inbox. This chapter discusses the third *D* in the 3D Approach—what to do about deferred emails. To help with this, I'll be introducing a simple yet effective planning and productivity tool.

Task-related emails are not prioritized in our inbox, and their deadlines are not obvious. For this reason and more, we need to move these task-related emails out of our inbox, but we also need to be confident we won't forget about them, which is a valid concern.

Email Warriors do not treat their inbox as if it were a to-do list. Rather, if a task arrives via email that they cannot complete in the short term, they make note of the task on a central list. Then they move the email out of their inbox (by either storing or deleting it) so it does not clog their inbox. To effectively manage our priorities, we all need a central record of all outstanding tasks, deadlines, goals and commitments. Our inbox is not suited to this task. We need a plan. We need a Master Plan.

The power of a Master Plan

Your Master Plan is essentially a to-do list. But it is not like typical to-do lists, which tend to get a bad rap. Most to-do lists are ineffective because they are outdated, incomplete, overwhelming or messy. People compensate by creating new lists and adding more systems. This complicates their planning process and often makes them become reactive instead of proactive. They end up scrambling to stay on top of everything and playing a perpetual game of catch-up.

In contrast, your Master Plan is the best to-do list you have ever seen. Calling this system a Master Plan reflects the strategic role this list plays in your life. Your Master Plan is a sophisticated, critical tool, which allows you to track your tasks, prioritize your work and manage expectations. And for Email Warriors, a Master Plan helps them to keep their inbox clear.

Track tasks with your Master Plan

While many tasks come in via email, many others arise from meetings, projects, phone calls and your own goals. A Master Plan allows you to corral all of the disparate tasks you cannot tackle today into one central system. When you centralize your outstanding tasks, you eliminate the nagging feeling you are forgetting about something. You avoid the embarrassment associated with people following up with you after the deadline has passed. You become more organized, which helps to cut down on feelings of overwhelm associated with the sheer volume of tasks. There is something both refreshing and empowering about having to look in only one place to see all of your outstanding work.

Most importantly, a Master Plan means you don't need to keep all of the outstanding "task" emails in your inbox. You can move them into folders or archives and note the task on your Master Plan. A Master Plan provides you with a much better system than email to track your work. It also allows you to clear the clutter out of your inbox. And even more critical, a Master Plan allows you to prioritize your tasks and attach deadlines, which you cannot do in your inbox.

Prioritize work with your Master Plan

As a busy person with many things on the go, you need to be crystal clear about your top priorities, so you can focus most of your attention on them. Clarity drives focus. And focus drives progress. A Master Plan helps you identify, focus on and make rapid progress on your most important work.

"When everything is a priority, nothing is a priority."
—Simon Fulleringer

Without a Master Plan, we often lull ourselves into believing we have more clarity than we actually do. But there is no way we can accurately compare and rank this many tasks in our head or when they are scattered across various list-making tools, including our inbox. Only when we have corralled all of our tasks can we clearly determine our top priority.

Manage expectations with your Master Plan

Once you have corralled all of your commitments into one place, you can better gauge your capacity. This helps you understand when you need to say no to lower-priority requests. It also helps you to commit to deadlines with more awareness about what is attainable. This greatly improves your follow-through and collaboration with other people.

Without a solid priority management system, many people over-promise and under-deliver. They end up acting like the proverbial kid in a candy store, jumping from one treat to the next, feeling torn while they wonder whether another sugary treat (or another pressing task) would have been a better choice. This behaviour generally does not stem from a malicious intent, but instead from a poor understanding of their capacity given competing deadlines.

> "Your mind is for having ideas, not holding them."
> —David Allen

When we try to tackle too many priorities at once, we get caught up in all of the associated emails, meetings, independent work, and so on. As we all know, "When everything is a priority, nothing is a priority."[1] We can't tackle umpteen projects all at the same time, nor can we keep up with all of their associated emails.

Why not to rely on your memory

Your memory is *not* your to-do list. Moving a task-related email out of your inbox should *not* mean you are now relying on your memory. That would not be fair to you or to others. Even if you remember practically everything, you likely won't remember it at the right time. People often overestimate what they can remember and forget things they swear they will not. Anyone who has woken up in the middle of the night with the dreaded realization they forgot to do something can relate to this.

Busy people cannot possibly rely on their memory alone to remember all of their commitments (or at least cannot do so in an efficient way). So do yourself a favour: do not even try. As productivity guru David Allen wisely said: "Your mind is for having ideas, not holding them." Our brains are simply not designed to function as to-do lists. A Master Plan compensates for our limited short-term memory. Our short-term memory is designed to help us recall a select number of things, while dedicating the rest of its capacity to working through problems. A landmark 1956 paper by George A. Miller of Princeton University introduced Miller's Law, which says we can hold merely seven objects (plus or minus two) in our working memory at one time.[2] According to folklore, this is the reason why phone numbers were originally designed to be seven digits long.[3]

More recent research indicates that our working memory capacity may be even less than we originally assumed. An updated estimate indicates we can keep between three and five chunks of information in our short-term memory as adults (and even fewer as children and older adults).[4] Returning to the phone number concept, it seems we remember certain things in groups. For example, the three numbers that make up a familiar area code are considered one "chunk" of information we can remember.

To make matters worse, our short-term memory is impeded by both aging and stress. Normal aging leads to diminished memory abilities, known as age-related memory impairment (AMI).[5] Stress does have the benefit of enabling us to focus our energy on the imminent threat. However, chronic stress can have a negative impact on our memory, among other things. An excess of the stress hormone cortisol prevents the hippocampus from storing new memories and retrieving existing memories.[6] Stress also seems to accelerate aging in the brain, leading to deterioration in the hippocampus and frontal cortex, the precise areas that help with memory.[7] But barring a diagnosed memory impairment, the real problem lies in the fact that we try to remember too many things.

What about those born with a photographic memory? As it turns out, truly photographic memories (technically referred to as eidetic memories) are a myth. Of course, some people exhibit better memories than others.[8]

Inevitably, tasks get overlooked when we try to remember too many details. And remembering only some (or even most) of our tasks is not acceptable in the workplace. Even if we remember 90 percent of our commitments, other people are counting on us for the remaining 10 percent. In the professional world, follow-through is expected to hit close to 100 percent. Clearly we need a better system than relying on our memory.

Your most important productivity tool

A Master Plan is your most critical productivity tool. It is the foundation from which all other productivity principles are built. A Master Plan allows you to track your tasks, prioritize your work and manage expectations. And as an Email Warrior, it allows you to clear your inbox without forgetting about key work. The next chapter will help you build this key productivity tool: a Master Plan customized to fit your unique style. Allow yourself a small amount of time to invest in developing this powerful system and then commit to using it every day. Once you have adopted a Master Plan, I guarantee you won't look back.

IV

Becoming an Email Warrior

11

Step 1: Build Your Master Plan

As you read in the previous chapter, your Master Plan is much like a to-do list—only much, much better. It is a strategic tool that tracks your tasks, prioritizes your work and manages expectations. You likely already have a system (or several systems) to track your work. However, there may be room for improvement in your system. This chapter shows you how to refine your current system into a solid Master Plan that suits your individual style. Then you will be ready to clear your inbox.

Setting up a Master Plan requires a small amount of

your time but boosts your productivity tremendously. In approximately 30 minutes, you can create an extremely effective Master Plan, which can then be seamlessly integrated into how you manage your work, including your email. The late educator Stephen R. Covey talked about sharpening the saw (see sidebar) to illustrate the importance of investing in yourself.[1] Establishing your Master Plan is the most effective way to sharpen your saw, increase your productivity and help keep your inbox clear.

Five critical features of your Master Plan

The following list sets out the five critical features of a Master Plan. Namely, it should be complete, centralized, categorized, committed and consulted. In other words, an ideal Master Plan aligns to the five Cs. As you read this list, consider how your existing system aligns with these features and what you can do to enhance your system.

- *Complete.* Your Master Plan should capture *all* of your tasks, commitments, deadlines and goals. Commit to writing down everything, and resist trying to rely on your memory (for reasons outlined on page 110). Once you have compiled a complete list of all outstanding work, you can effectively compare and prioritize your tasks. Without a single complete list, you may find yourself jumping from one urgent task

Sharpen your saw

As the story goes, there were two woodsmen chopping down trees. The first woodsman worked relentlessly all day long, without taking a break. Every once in a while he glanced over at the second woodsman, who seemed to take one break after another to sit down on a tree stump. At the end of the day, they each counted up the number of trees they had cut down. Surprisingly, the second woodsman (who took frequent breaks) had cut down far more trees. The first woodsman was flabbergasted. "How could this be possible?" he asked his fellow woodsman. "Every time I looked over, you were sitting down!" The second woodsman calmly answered: "Yes, but every time I sat down, I sharpened my saw."[2] What can you do to pause and sharpen your saw? If necessary, I suggest you start by sharpening your Master Plan.

to another. You might feel perpetually behind in your work and frustrated that there isn't enough of you to go around. Without a complete list, you might find yourself overcommitted and inevitably late on delivering work to other people. Such behaviour prevents you from making meaningful progress on your true priorities. Does any of this ring true for you?

- *Centralized.* Most people rely on too many disjointed, unorganized systems to track their priorities. They use sticky notes surrounding their computer monitor and notes piled up underneath. They flag emails and mark messages as unread. They create handwritten lists and electronic lists. They use apps and they rely on their memory. They also use piles of paper or rely on other people to remind them of tasks. One client even admitted that if other people don't come back to him a second time for something, they didn't really need it in the first place, which strikes me as a weak system at best.

A Master Plan allows you to delete or file any associated emails and do the same with any associated paper. On the other hand, relying on multiple task-tracking systems is a method doomed to fail. The more systems we have, the more places we need to look. This can lead to things getting overlooked, time being wasted, and that nagging feeling that we just don't have a handle on everything. Instead, focus on establishing one central system where you collect all of your plans, goals, commitments and deadlines.

What to capture?

Question: Should *everything* go on my Master Plan? What about all the details from business plans and project plans? Answer: Your Master Plan should capture high-level ideas from your business plan, which you can flesh out in more detail as the goals become more immediate. Your Master Plan should also capture immediate action items from a project plan (but not the entire project plan). Immediate project-related tasks need to be consolidated in the same list as all of your other work so you can prioritize your work. Note that you do not to need to transfer others' tasks from a project plan to your Master Plan. Assuming you have a system in place to regularly review the project plans (such as regular team meetings), there is no need for a redundant system. (For more on this topic, see the section "How to track delegated tasks," page 129.)

Everything you need to do goes on one central list. Let go of any other task-tracking systems and commit to using your Master Plan consistently.

- *Categorized.* Your Master Plan includes a wide range of tasks that should be categorized according to common themes. We all have different types of work (e.g., clients, team, business development, personal, and so on), and each category has its own priorities and tasks. Grouping our tasks by category allows us to easily rank related work.

> "A goal is a dream with a deadline."
>
> —Napoleon Hill

Prioritizing tasks within a category makes sense, whereas prioritizing tasks across categories does not. Comparing a client priority to a personal priority is like comparing apples to oranges. Each category has its own unique goals and warrants its own dedicated time.

Streamline your work by limiting the number of your categories on your Master Plan. I recommend no more than four categories. I recently consolidated two of my categories to simplify my priority management system. I now work with three categories instead of four. In your case, you might find that two, three or four categories is the best balance.

- *Committed.* The best way to commit to a task is to add a deadline. In the wise words of Napoleon Hill, a twentieth-century American author who produced some of the earliest personal-success literature,

"A goal is a dream with a deadline." Alternatively, what happens when we do not set ourselves deadlines? According to Parkinson's Law, "Work expands to fill the time available for its completion."

Without a doubt, we are more committed to tasks when they have a deadline firmly attached. Deadlines reinforce our commitment and keep us focused on our top-priority tasks. The lack of a deadline is one of the main causes of procrastination, so it is to our benefit to add a deadline to anything we intend to complete.

External deadlines can be very effective. When possible, tell someone else you will get something done by a specific date. Avoid "as soon as possible" or "when I can" commitments, which often lead to tasks sitting on your to-do list for far too long. You also want to be specific about what you are committing to do. Break down big projects into smaller, attainable steps and assign a deadline to each step. List your action items in a very specific way, beginning with a verb. For example: "Summarize quarterly results" is a much more effective task than simply listing "Budget" as your task. The more specific you are, the more focused you become.

- *Consulted.* This is by far the most important feature of your Master Plan. At risk of stating the obvious, you need to *consult* your Master Plan on a daily basis. You should add things to the list and cross them off in real time. (Is it just me, or is the latter one of life's simple pleasures?) Updating your Master Plan should take you practically no time, since you are thinking of the task anyways. This update should become part of your task management ritual and not an activity you leave till the end of the day.

  Consulting (and updating) your Master Plan is best done in real time because otherwise, your plan becomes outdated almost immediately and tasks will be forgotten. Then all your work in setting up your Master Plan has to be recreated. If I had a nickel for every time I saw someone let this happen, I'd be one rich woman. Make no mistake: this is the most important of the five Cs.

Sample Master Plan

This sample Master Plan has clear tasks in two simple categories. It lists deadlines on the left, ranked in order of due date. Tasks are specific, briefly worded (starting with a verb) and focused on outcomes.

PROJECTS	TEAM
Jan. 9: Update Jones	Jan. 12: Secure venue for event
Jan. 11: Finalize presentation	Jan. 30: Book debrief
Jan. 16: Send Thomson letter	Feb. 7: Finalize agenda
Jan. 27: Prepare for meeting	
Feb. 3: Finalize Huron report	

Customize your Master Plan

You may absolutely customize your Master Plans to fit your personal preferences. Effective plans come in many different shapes and sizes. Regardless of what your Master Plan looks like, it should adhere to the five Cs. It should be complete, centralized and categorized. You should add a commitment (deadline) to every task and consult it on a daily basis (or even more often, as the need arises).

Here are some of the many format options to consider as you create (or refine) your Master Plan, ranging from low-tech (handwritten) to virtual (cloud-based). Pick the option that resonates most with you and your unique working preferences.

- *Word processing program.* Many people create their Master Plans using a word processor such as Microsoft Word or Google Docs. People tend to be comfortable working with these programs and they can keep their list readily accessible on their computer, which enables them to keep it current in real time. The only drawback is that this system is not always readily accessible when you are away from your computer (unless you print a copy or save it in the cloud, which are both workable solutions).

- *Application.* Countless applications are available to help track one's tasks. Each of them offers slightly different features, so you'll have to spend a few minutes comparing features to pick the one you like the best. You could consider using a dedicated list-making tool such as Evernote. Or your might prefer to use a task-tracking application such as Wunderlist. Dedicated applications do an excellent job of sorting your tasks by deadline. Both list-making tools and task-tracking applications synch up your computer, tablet, smartphone, and so on. This gives you access to your Master Plan anytime you are within reach of one of these devices and thus enables you to keep it current.

- *Email software.* Many email systems, such as Microsoft Outlook, Lotus Notes, Apple Mail and Gmail, have task management systems that synchronize with your email. These systems typically allow you to drag and drop emails into the task management system, which can be very handy (especially given that many tasks arrive via email). They also typically synchronize very well to your smartphone or tablet, which keeps your Master Plan always easily accessible.

However, be wary of the multiple bells and whistles associated with these tools. For reasons outlined above, it's best to keep your Master Plan simple. All you need to note is the specific task, due date and category. Then be sure to rank your tasks within each category by due date. There is no need to use all the other available features, such as percent completion and level of urgency. Rather, you will use deadlines to rank tasks by priority.

- *Handwritten list.* There are still some die-hards who love their handwritten lists. I can appreciate that many people like to work with a physical piece of paper where they can write down new tasks and cross things off as they are completed. There is some evidence that actually writing things down helps us to remember them more so than typing them does.[3]

Although I prefer to see people using electronic lists, a handwritten list can work as a Master Plan—as long as it aligns with the five Cs listed earlier in this chapter. If you like to use a handwritten list, I suggest you set it up electronically and then print it. That way, you are working with your preferred paper version, but avoiding the redundancy of recreating your entire list when the paper version becomes too marked up. Your paper version will (and should) get marked up with new tasks and crossed-off tasks. Therefore, you should plan to periodically (say, weekly) update your electronic list and print a new copy.

I used to use this system, since I loved having a physical copy of my Master Plan. There was something about the tangible piece of paper that gave me comfort. But I'll be honest, I didn't get around to updating my electronic copy often enough. And when my paper version got too marked up, it became tougher to read and thus less effective. Once I faced this fact, I transitioned over to a pure electronic list that I can access from both my computer and my phone. Although the new system took a bit of getting used to, I've come to love my always-current electronic list.

As you can see, you have a number of format options to consider when customizing your Master Plan. Choose one that best suits your style, and try it for at least a month. That should provide you with enough time to adopt the habit. At the end of that period, evaluate whether your Master Plan aligns with the five Cs and is also working well for you. If necessary, try using another system, until you find one that fits with your unique work style.

Your Master Plan: What *not* to use

By now you know that your inbox should not function as your to-do list. You also know that your memory is not a fail-safe system. Several other systems also fail to prioritize your work, such as to-do folders, your calendar and flagged emails. Here's why.

- *To-do folders.* I do not suggest you set up a to-do folder in your email program. Email messages in folders such as this can get forgotten far too quickly. Time is limited, and in my experience, people rarely make time to work through a non-urgent "miscellaneous" folder like this.
- *Your calendar.* No question, your calendar is a critical tool to track all of your appointments, meetings and blocked time. However, your calendar is not your to-do list. The problem with using your calendar to track deadlines is you cannot view all work in one central place. Hence you lose the ability to compare and prioritize your tasks.

  Tracking tasks in your calendar also leads to wasted time spent scrolling through your calendar to look at the various tasks. People compensate by adding reminders, but they often end up dismissing them with little thought when they pop up at an inopportune time. This defeats the purpose of the reminder in the first place. Instead of doing its job, the reminder often serves as a distraction, prompting multi-tasking and higher anxiety.

To reiterate an important point: your calendar is a critical tool for tracking meetings and appointments. However, if you have a task associated with that meeting, you should note that on your Master Plan (for example, Prepare for meeting). Your calendar tells you to *go* to the meeting. Your Master Plan tells you to *prepare* for the meeting.

- *Flagged emails.* Do you ever flag emails or mark them as unread? Unfortunately, doing this creates chaos in your inbox and in no way prioritizes your tasks. Flagging emails or marking them as unread ("to act on" later) adds an unnecessary step and does not guarantee you will come back to the email if it is more than one screen down. Instead, simply leave emails you plan to act on in the *immediate short term* in your inbox. But allow only a few emails to remain in your inbox. If you do not plan to act on the email in the short term, file it away, and make a note on your Master Plan so you don't forget the item.

How to track delegated tasks

When you supervise people or collaborate on projects, you need a system to track delegated work. This may be a separate category in your Master Plan or an appendix to your Master Plan. You can also use this system to track items you want to review with other people at upcoming meetings.

For any pending tasks related to your work, add them to your own Master Plan. For example, you could add a note to follow up with a client if you don't hear back from them by Friday.

Sample list of pending tasks

Here is an example of a pending tasks tracker, which you can treat as an appendix to your Master Plan. Note again the precise wording of these tasks, beginning with a verb. Where appropriate, add deadlines to these pending tasks and list them by date.

Kelly—Delegated Tasks	François—Delegated Tasks
• Complete trademark application • Finalize conference details	• Update precedence • Prepare board meeting agenda
Items to Discuss • Client tracker updates	**Items to Discuss** • Team meeting follow-up

Daily planning

Although your Master Plan captures everything you need to do, you likely need a bring-forward version to run your day. You need a daily plan. This is a brief list of what you plan to do today. You could capture this list electronically or using a small notepad. If you use a notepad, be sure to get rid of the paper at the end of the day. It is not a collector's item. As well, try to limit the number of tasks on your daily plan to a maximum of five, so you feel a sense of accomplishment after crossing off most if not all items by the end of the day. Consider how much discretionary time you have to work before adding tasks to your daily plan. All other tasks should go on your Master Plan. If you finish all of the tasks on your daily plan, you can always go back to your Master Plan. Finally, strive to plan for the next day as you are wrapping up your work each day, so you can jump right into your first task the following morning.

Sample daily plan

1. Prepare for meeting
2. Review document

- Call John
- Submit application
- Book dentist

Email Warrior Action Plan Step 1: Build Your Master Plan

Estimated time to complete: 30 minutes
To recap, your Master Plan will capture all of your tasks, commitments, deadlines and goals in one place. It will be complete, centralized, categorized, committed and consulted. Build your Master Plan by following these simple steps:

- *Start with why.* Remind yourself that your Master Plan will help you clear your inbox. It will also help you prioritize your work, manage expectations and make sure nothing gets forgotten. Clearly, this is an important tool.
- *Pick your system.* Consider how you currently track your tasks. Are you relying on one central system or are you relying on multiple systems? Which one seems to work best for you?
- *Centralize and categorize.* Pull all of your tasks and deadlines together on one central list. Organize everything in approximately three categories (potentially for both work and home).

- *Add deadlines*. Add due dates to all tasks. Where none exist, create your own deadlines. Going forward, add a deadline for every new task. Rank all tasks according to their deadline.
- *Commit to your system*. Commit to using your new system exclusively and write down all of your tasks. Retire any other systems (including making lists in spiral-bound notebooks, flagging emails and using your memory).

Now that you have a great Master Plan in place, you are one step closer to clearing your inbox. The next step is to streamline your email storage system, which you will learn about in the next chapter. Hang in there; you are so close to becoming an Email Warrior and radically changing how you work.

12

Step 2: Streamline Your Storage System

Your ultimate goal is to move emails out of your inbox. This chapter addresses *where* to move emails that you have acted on or need to process in the future. In essence, you have three options: you can file them, archive them or delete them. The key is to know when to use each strategy.

Obviously, we know to delete the emails we will never look at again. At the other end of the spectrum, there are some emails we absolutely want to keep. But in between is a fuzzy middle ground full of emails that often get left in our inbox. Establishing a workable filing system will help you determine what to keep and where. As you already know from chapter 6, most people keep far more emails than they need. That's why it's important to purge as many as you can. The more emails you purge, the easier it is to comb through them to find the critical ones worth finding again.

Some emails contain critical details we need for current or future projects. Others contain important reference information. There may also be the occasional feel-good email you want to hold onto for good memories. But as you know by now, you do not want to keep these emails in your inbox. Instead, set up an email storage system that will enable you to organize key messages for ready access.

This storage system will have the added benefit of lowering your stress. Research conducted by Professor Tom Jackson and his team at Loughborough University found that filing emails into folders lowers stress levels and helps people feel in control.[1] Although this intuitively makes sense, such research validates the process of filing email.

This chapter explains how to set up an effective email storage system by following these steps:

- *Actively purge emails.* Recognize that you likely won't look at many emails again. Push yourself to purge all emails that you don't anticipate referring to again.

- *Select your reference system.* Decide whether you will use a filing or archiving system for all emails that you *do* want to keep.
- *Streamline your folder structure.* Where appropriate, establish primary folders and nest other folders as necessary.
- *Commit to moving emails.* Whenever you are processing emails, commit to getting them out of your inbox using the One-Touch Principle (see chapter 9). Do this as you go. Don't wait for the end of the day or end of the week to move emails out of your inbox.

Filing versus archiving

What does the ideal storage system look like? There are two options to consider: filing and archiving. A filing system consists of folders dedicated to different topics. Filing allows you to move emails out of your inbox and into folders, where you can group related information. Folders allow you to sort through fewer emails on a related topic when looking to retrieve information. Email systems like Outlook and Lotus offer folders, whereas other email programs, such as Google Mail (Gmail), allow you to work with labels, which can function in a similar way to folders.

An archive system,[2] as compared to a filing system, still allows you to access old emails, but it doesn't store emails by categories. For example, in Gmail, an archived

Document management systems

Some organizations require their employees to save key emails in a document management system (DMS). Often, these systems operate similarly to a filing system, but they are external to the email system. A DMS is often designed to prompt information sharing across teams and mitigate risk of data loss. A DMS also helps to preserve institutional knowledge, regardless of how the team changes over time.

email gets labelled as "All Mail" and is no longer visible in your inbox (although retrievable by searching within the "All Mail" label). It is as if archived emails go into one big bucket that is distinct from your inbox. Searching for keywords, names, and so on usually does a very good job of pulling up the information you are looking for within such archive systems.

Archiving makes it very easy to remove emails from your inbox. You don't have to decide where to put the email—you simply archive it. Some people claim that with ongoing improvements to search functionality, folders will eventually be phased out in favour of archiving. In the meantime, there is still a large population of folder enthusiasts.

What choice is the best for you?

If you like your information logically grouped by topics, filing is likely the best approach for you. On the other hand, if you are comfortable performing searches and are reluctant to subdivide emails into different folders, archiving can be a much more streamlined approach.

I'll admit I am still a fan of folders. I find sorting emails by folders makes it much easier to find project-specific messages. At work, I have folders for different projects, colleagues, clients, and so on. In my personal life, I have folders for the kids' activities, family vacations, friends, and online shopping receipts. I am not as comfortable with solely relying on searches. Despite advances in search functionality, I cannot get around the fact that the more emails I accumulate, the more hits a search will find. Folders, on the other hand, clearly organize information you might otherwise have forgotten to search for.

Although search enthusiasts might disagree, most times I find it easier to locate information by searching in dedicated folders than through general searches. Perhaps, over time (and with ever-improving search functionality), I'll be convinced to move to an archive system. The simplicity of archiving holds definite appeal.

Some people prefer a blended option. They have largely given up on folders, although still like to keep certain emails (and know that it doesn't work to keep them in their inbox). Instead of using multiple folders, they use just one folder, which they call "Reference" or "Keep." Or they might have a few select main folders such as "Clients," "Team," "Colleagues," and "Marketing," for example. They toss any emails they want to keep into the main folder(s). Emails are thus moved out of their inbox but are still accessible. This is an effective strategy for anyone comfortable using searches within these broader folders.

Folders: Where people go wrong

There is a good chance that you are already using folders. However, you may be experiencing some "folder frustration." When a folder structure is not easy to work with, people often end up leaving emails in their inbox (which you know by now is not the way to go). Here are several common mistakes to avoid when setting up your folders.

- *Too many folders.* An excess of folders makes it cumbersome to scroll through the loooong list to find the right one. With too many folders, you'll also have too many places to look, which can be a frustrating time drain. As well, the more folders you have, the more likely something will get misplaced.
- *No folder groupings.* Individual folders are often listed alphabetically based on default email settings.

What about automatic filing?

Some people automatically file certain emails into pre-established folders as they arrive. This certainly saves their inbox from getting full. And it also allows people to batch-process related messages. If you do this, just make sure you dedicate the time to actually work through these folders. I can't tell you how many people don't take the time to sort through the messages in these folders. When you don't see them, it's as if the emails were never sent to you. For this reason, I tend not to be an advocate of automatic email filing. If you don't regularly check the related folders, I would rather see your emails landing in your inbox, where you can decide what to do with them.

Outdated folders housing long-forgotten projects may end up ranking higher than the new hot project you work on every single day.

- *Date-stamped folders.* Some people set up folders to represent periods of time. The problem is, we remember things better by subject matter rather than the date we worked on them.

- *People-stamped folders.* Some people set up a folder for every individual they work with. But what happens when an email relates to multiple people? It is often easier to file emails by project. Clearly, there are some exceptions. For example, you might want a dedicated folder for your manager and each team member when you want to save messages specifically related to these people.

How to streamline your folders

Based on what I've seen across hundreds of inboxes, many folder structures could use a good ol' spring cleaning. Streamlining your folders is a critical step in the journey towards becoming an Email Warrior. After all, your reference system is a critical tool in managing your digital information. Once you have a solid email reference system, you'll find it easier to move emails out of your inbox and pinpoint key information as necessary.

Thankfully, streamlining your folders is a fairly straightforward and quick process. You just need to follow three simple steps, namely (1) Establish your primary folders, (2) Nest your secondary folders, and (3) Update your folder structure as necessary. Plan to dedicate approximately 15 minutes to this task, and you will recoup that investment in no time.

Step 1. Establish your primary folders

The first step is to identify your primary folders. These represent your main categories of work and might be subjects such as clients, team, projects, and so on. Here are some things to keep in mind when establishing your primary folders.

- *Sort by topic.* We tend to look for information associated with a particular topic, and our folder structure should be based

> "Simplicity is the ultimate sophistication."
> —Leonardo da Vinci

on this. Generally, I recommend one folder per client or project (unless there is a definitive reason to subdivide further). You have multiple search functionalities that can help you zero in on the correct message within each folder. For example, you can search by subject line, names and keywords. You can also scroll down to the appropriate date range within each folder to find the email you are looking for.
- *Less is more.* Aim for about 8 to 15 main folders. Any more than this and your filing system starts to get too complicated. Most people have far too many folders, which complicates things. *Should I put the email in this folder or that folder?*

- *Make topics stand out.* I recommend using ALL CAPS when naming primary folders. We want these primary folders to be easy to find and stand out from any of the nested folders.
- *Force the ranking.* Most email systems automatically list the folders in alphabetical order. The easiest way to get around this is to number your folders. By doing so, you get to decide their order. Put your most frequently used folders at the top of your list.
- *Recycle existing folders.* You likely already have many of these main folders in your existing list of folders. You can simply rename these existing folders to align with the above file structure.

Sample primary folder structure

1. ACTIVE CLIENTS
2. TEAM
3. PROJECTS
4. COLLEAGUES
5. PROGRAMS
6. RESEARCH
7. ADMIN
8. PERSONAL

Step 2. Nest your secondary folders

You may want to have some specific folders dedicated to individual clients, team members, projects, and so on. You can create secondary folders for each of these and nest them under your primary folders. With this nesting approach, related folders are now grouped together. This keeps your information organized and easier to navigate.

Most email systems allow you to collapse (or hide) your nested folders. This allows you to navigate through a streamlined list of primary folders. Your folder structure is simple and clear, which makes organizing your digital information so much easier. And you can easily expand your list if necessary.

Sample nested folders

 3.   PROJECTS
        Client event
        New branding
        Team offsite
        Book tour
        Trademarks

Step 3. Update your folder structure as necessary

Don't be afraid to move your folders as necessary. As your work evolves, your folder needs will also change. As well, if any of your folder lists gets too long, you might split out the active folders from the inactive folders. On that note, I keep an "Active Clients" folder as well as a "Former Clients" folder. When a former client becomes an active client again, I can easily move their folder back under the "Active Clients" primary folder.

Once you have a streamlined folder structure, you are much better prepared to keep your inbox clear. These well-organized "homes" (folders) make it so much easier to clear out emails from your inbox throughout the day. All of this preparation supports your ultimate goal: clearing your inbox. Let's go.

Email Warrior Action Plan Step 2: Streamline Your Storage System

Estimated time to complete: 15 minutes
Streamline your storage system by following these steps:

- *Actively purge emails.* Recognize that you likely won't look at many emails again. Push yourself to purge all emails that you don't anticipate referring to again.
- *Select your reference system.* Decide whether you will use a filing or archiving system for all emails that you do want to keep.
- *Streamline your folder structure.* Where appropriate, establish primary folders and nest other folders as necessary.
- *Commit to moving emails.* When processing emails, commit to moving messages out of your inbox as you apply the One-Touch Principle throughout the day.

13

Step 3: Clear Your Inbox

This is the most exciting chapter because you are only a few steps away from the liberating feeling of a clear inbox. The weight of hundreds or even thousands of emails is about to be lifted off of your shoulders. Digital clutter will no longer drag you down.

The task of scrolling through 700 emails or 7,000 emails or even 77,000 emails may feel insurmountable. However, this challenge is not as daunting as it appears, regardless of your current inbox count. Do not worry if you have countless emails in your inbox. This chapter walks you through a relatively painless way to clear out that backlog. All you need to do is dedicate some time to make it happen.

Clearing your inbox does require uninterrupted focus time. So find a relatively clear slot in your calendar to focus on this important task. I recommend blocking off two hours. If you are having trouble finding the time, remind yourself that you often give away your time to other people. You deserve to take this time for yourself, especially considering the high return on investment (ROI) you will receive. Pick a time when you will not face distractions and the tug towards other work. A Monday morning or the day before the big deal closes likely won't give you the protected time you need. Find a quiet location that enables you to truly immerse yourself in this task. Obviously, you can build in a break, but I recommend trying to complete this process in one shot as opposed to spreading it out over several days. Hunker down and clear your inbox. Then, going forward, use the 3D Approach to keep your inbox clear..

This chapter relies on work you have already completed, as described in previous chapters. Ask yourself the following questions before attempting to clear your inbox:

- *Do I have a Master Plan? (chapter 11).* You need to have one central system in place to track all of your tasks, deadlines, commitments and goals. When you have a great Master Plan in place, you can feel confident in moving tasks out of your inbox and noting them on your Master Plan. If you don't have a reliable Master Plan, you will be reluctant to file or delete the email.

- *Do I have a streamlined digital storage system? (chapter 12).* You also need a storage system for any messages you want to keep that is well organized and easy to use. Unless you know where to put things, it will be hard to file them away. Even one general reference folder is better than keeping everything in your inbox.
- *Have I adopted the One-Touch Principle? (chapter 9).* You need to process email in the most efficient manner to keep up with the volume and avoid having email consume your entire day. You also need to apply these efficient email habits to clear your inbox in the most streamlined manner.

Assuming the above three critical pieces are in place, you are ready to clear your inbox. So let's get to work. To clear your inbox, follow a few straightforward steps:

- *Archive old messages.* Move all emails older than six weeks old into an archive, folder or label called "Sort." If you are dealing with thousands of emails, move them in batches. Resist the temptation to actually sort through these old messages at this time.

- *Work through your recent emails.* Commit to clearing out your recent emails from your inbox. Start with your least current (i.e., six weeks old) and move forward in time sequentially.
- *Do it or defer it.* For every email, choose to either do the task right then or defer the task, adding it to your Master Plan. In both situations, move the email out of your inbox afterwards.
- *Reward yourself.* Once you've cleared your inbox, give yourself a reward. After all, this is a big deal.

We will begin this process with the step that will have the biggest impact—getting rid of any outdated backlog.

First, clear out old messages

The secret to clearing your inbox in less than two hours is to focus exclusively on your most recent emails. Begin by removing the vast majority of older emails. Take any emails more than six weeks old and park them in a "Sort" folder. In one fell swoop, you will be able to clear out countless dusty old emails.

Now, to be clear, I'm not actually encouraging you to sort through these older emails. At least I don't recommend you do that right now. Remind yourself that you weren't doing anything with these older emails when they were buried at the bottom of your inbox. You could call this folder "I'll never look at these again," which is probably a better description. The key is to get these emails out of your inbox. And these older emails will always be available in your "Sort" folder if you need them again.

Focusing on your most recent emails is justified, since emails tend to have a short life. Anything older than six weeks is a dinosaur in the digital age. Don't let your momentum fade and distractions get in your way. Allow yourself to make this process as easy as possible.

If you insist on actually sorting through these old emails, you can absolutely go back and do so. However, commit to doing this only *after* clearing out your recent emails. And even then, spend only a small amount of time doing this old sort. Those emails are not going anywhere once you move them into a "Sort" folder or label. The safety net is there if you need it.

Tip: Move only a few hundred emails at a time. The process will go relatively quickly, even if you have tens of thousands of emails sitting in your inbox. If you move more than a few hundred at a time, your computer may become sluggish or freeze. And then you might be tempted to send me hate mail. Or even worse, hate email.

A life-changing journey

Mark walked out of my Email Warrior workshop determined to clear his inbox. He was sick of feeling as though email was holding him hostage, with more than 20,000 messages clogging his inbox. He hopped on a plane from Toronto to Vancouver determined to make this happen. By the time he landed, he was a whole new person, with fewer than ten emails in his inbox. And while that life-changing plane ride was several years ago, he still abides by the Email Warrior approach.

Next, clear your recent emails

Now that you have archived all of your old emails, you can focus your attention on your most recent emails. By the end of this step, you will have reduced your inbox to fewer than ten emails. You are almost there.

Start with the least current

When you are clearing out your recent emails, start with your least current messages (i.e., those from six weeks ago). Move sequentially through your messages, dealing with each email in turn. Try to avoid jumping to the easy ones, which simply prolongs the harder work and invites you to procrastinate on the harder emails. I once heard we are more likely to procrastinate every time we face a decision point in our day, so remove the decision associated with which email to look at next. To repeat: Sequentially process your email, beginning with the least current.

The only exception to this sequential approach would be if you come across an email that is related to several other emails sitting in your inbox. In this case, you might want to sort by subject line, by sender or by keywords. This can help you move multiple related emails to a project-specific folder in one step. Then reset your inbox and go back to processing the least current emails.

Tip: You will always face new emails vying for your attention. Resist the urge to tackle today's emails during this session. If you get sidetracked by the new emails, you might never find the time to clear out the old emails.

Make one of two choices

As you sequentially process your recent messages, your goal is to clear each and every email out of your inbox. Remember, for every email, you have two choices: to do (act on it now) or to defer (act on it later). To review, these strategies are covered in more depth in chapters 9 and 10:

- *Do it.* Use the One-Touch Principle to process the email. Take whatever action the email justifies. Read it; reply to it; forward it; and so on. Do what you need to do to *get it done.* Avoid considering whether you feel like doing it now. It is the next email on the list and therefore the next email to process. Once you have acted on it, get it out of your inbox. Delete, file or archive the message. Then move on to the next email.

- *Defer it.* Some emails simply cannot be dealt with right now. They might require too much work and will therefore pull you away from your current goal of clearing your inbox. Or you might need more information before you can process the email. If you can reach out to someone for some information or book a meeting to discuss the issue, do that now. But the original email still remains to be dealt with. The key is not to forget about it, but still to clear it out of your inbox.

This is where your Master Plan comes into play. Add the task to your Master Plan and add an appropriate deadline. You might even consider blocking time in your calendar to deal with the task. Now you can move the email out of your inbox without being concerned about forgetting to do the task. Delete, file or archive the message. When your Master Plan signals the task is a top priority, you can access the information from your digital storage system, as appropriate.

Exception: Short-term tasks

Admittedly, there is a small exception to the above choices. There might be a handful of emails you cannot act on right now, but which you plan to address very soon. Like this afternoon or tomorrow or the end of this week. I believe it is acceptable to leave a handful of emails like this in your inbox, assuming you truly intend on addressing them in the short term (i.e., this week).

Your inbox can function as a short-term task list, as long as you keep these emails at an absolute minimum. Treat this rule as the exception, not the norm. As soon as you lower your threshold for "what stays," your inbox size creeps up. Resist the temptation to keep more than a handful of emails, even for the short term, and strive to get your inbox down to fewer than ten emails by the end of the day.[1] Move any other tasks out of your inbox and onto your Master Plan.

Some people advocate keeping nothing in their inbox, an idea that is certainly appealing. However, I find that keeping a small number of emails provides just the right amount of pressure to process them and clear them out. With a goal to keep fewer than ten emails in your inbox, you are still motivated to process emails efficiently, while keeping your inbox (relatively) clear.

When you apply the disciplined approach outlined in this chapter and put into practise the 3D Approach to inbox management, you end up with only a handful of short-term tasks in your inbox. Nothing gets buried or forgotten about. You remain focused on top priorities and avoid getting bogged down in a cluttered inbox. And you can say goodbye to the feeling of overwhelm associated with having countless screens of email in your inbox.

Now you are ready for the 30-Day Email Warrior Challenge. This is the final step before fully claiming your Email Warrior title. This challenge will help you establish your Email Warrior habits, putting into practice all the principles covered in this book to maintain a clear inbox—always.

Email Warrior Action Plan Step 3: Clear Your Inbox

Estimated time to complete: 2 hours

Clear your inbox by following these steps:

- *Archive old messages.* Move all emails older than six weeks old into an archive or folder called "Sort." If you are dealing with thousands of emails, move them in batches. Resist the temptation to actually sort through these old messages at this time.

- *Work through your recent emails.* Commit to clearing out your recent emails from your inbox. Start with your least current (i.e., six weeks old) and move forward in time sequentially.

- *Do or defer.* For every email, choose to either do the task right then or defer the task, adding it to your Master Plan. In both situations, move the email out of your inbox afterwards.

- *Reward yourself.* Once you've cleared your inbox, give yourself a reward. After all, this is a big deal.

- *Commit to the Email Warrior 30-Day Challenge.* Commit to using all the principles covered in this book to maintain your clear inbox. Use the thirty-day challenge to help establish your Email Warrior habits.

14

Take the 30-Day Challenge

Congratulations! Your inbox is now clear. This is an amazing accomplishment and something to be proud of. Now let's make sure your inbox stays this way. It's time for the 30-Day Email Warrior Challenge. Your goal is to keep your inbox relatively clear for the next thirty days and beyond. Commit to using all the principles in this book to efficiently process email and clear each message from your inbox throughout the day. At the end of one month, this new habit will be well engrained. In fact, it might feel strange to operate in any other way.

Throughout this challenge, strive to keep your inbox at

less than ten emails total, including both read and unread emails. Although your inbox will grow throughout the day, use the 3D Approach to *decide* what action needs to be taken, and then to *do* that action or *defer* email and move long-term action items out of your inbox.

Some people set up a jumbo screen just for email. I've even seen people turn their monitors vertically so they can fit more emails on their screen. Regardless of how big your monitor is, strive to maintain fewer than ten emails in your inbox. Ideally, you should not have to scroll down to see all of the emails in your inbox.

When we keep fewer than ten emails in our inbox, individual action items do not get missed and we avoid contributing to our backlog. We make better decisions, stay more organized and end up spending *less* time on email. When we consistently maintain fewer than ten emails in our inbox, we are truly worthy of the title Email Warrior.

Focus on your top priorities

Unfortunately, you do not control what lands in your inbox. Not everything will be associated with your top priorities. As a result, you need to carefully guard the time you put into these less important requests. Avoid falling into the trap of feeling productive while working through low-priority items.

The key to staying on top of email is to recognize that you cannot do everything on the "nice to do" list. Perhaps earlier in your career you had time to look at every message that came your way. But the volume of information you receive has likely increased over the years. In reality, you must be prepared to quickly skim and/or delete lower-priority messages. Minimize time spent on these emails and dedicate your focus to top priorities.

If an email is not associated with your top priorities, it justifies only a quick glance or response. Then move it out of your inbox so you can focus on more important work. Making efficient decisions like this is imperative. Otherwise, email can consume your day and your inbox can quickly build up again. Email Warriors give each individual message the time it deserves—and only that much time—based on how highly it ranks on their list of priorities. In doing so, Email Warriors actually spend *less* time on email than their counterparts.

When lower-priority "nice to do" requests land in your inbox, here are some suggested strategies to avoid having them consume your day.

- Provide a quick response (and let people follow up if they want more details).
- Refer the sender to someone else.
- Delegate the task to someone else.

- Quickly scan and absorb the high-level information.
- Delay the request: Let the sender know you can't focus on this until a later date (e.g., 1 month, 3 months, or 6 months from now). If you commit to following up with them at this time, add this task to your Master Plan.
- Decline the request: Let the sender know you unfortunately cannot commit to this.
- Encourage people to book time with you to discuss an issue (and suggest a date in the future).
- Respond with a partial answer and tie in one of the above strategies to deal with the other part.

Overall, Email Warriors carefully manage the time they spend on email. And the key is to avoid spending too much time (if any) on low-priority messages.

How to recover if you get behind

As Email Warriors, we want to stay on top of our email. But we also want to dedicate the majority of our time to our top priorities. Unfortunately, these can feel like conflicting goals at times. Should we spend time clearing our inbox or shift to other work while our inbox grows?

Obviously, a deluge of emails can be a sign that you are overcommitted. When this is the case, you receive far more emails than you have time to process. A more sustainable approach is to be more ruthless about defining what you can and cannot tackle right now. How can you streamline, scale back and seek help on your current obligations? Perhaps it is possible to postpone or remove yourself from lower-priority projects. Alternatively, negotiate new deadlines so you can focus on higher-priority goals.

During this thirty-day challenge, you are bound to face some excessively busy days. These may include hours of back-to-back meetings, urgent requests, travel delays, project meltdowns and extra personal commitments. On days like this, it will be nearly impossible to clear your inbox. The only solace may be to recognize that everyone has days like this.

When this happens, set aside time to clear the backlog of messages and get back to the goal of fewer than ten emails in your inbox. Although you don't want to let your inbox creep back up, I also encourage you to keep this issue in perspective. The last thing you should be doing is sacrificing sleep to clear your inbox.

A bloated inbox such as the one we encounter when we have been away from work for days or weeks should be the exception, not the norm. If an overflowing inbox is a more chronic challenge for you, either push more tasks over to your to-do list or scale back your priorities. You may also need to delegate more work, reduce time spent in meetings and protect more time for email. The bottom line? If you find that your inbox starts to grow beyond a single screen, block off time to whittle it back down.

Congratulations! You are an Email Warrior

Once you have kept your inbox clear for thirty days, you have earned the right to call yourself an Email Warrior. More importantly, you will reap all of the associated benefits:

- *Tight backlog.* An overflowing inbox is often a sign of numerous unfinished tasks pending your decision or action. Alternatively, a relatively clear inbox is a sign of your success in maintaining a reasonable backlog.
- *Less time on email.* As an Email Warrior, you will spend less time on email overall. You will not face the follow-up emails asking "Have you had a chance to look at this yet?" Nor will you waste time scrolling through your inbox looking for messages that need your attention.
- *Better decision-making.* You will find yourself making more efficient decisions. After all, you don't want to leave that email sitting in your inbox. In the past, you might have let a decision percolate for a while. But rarely do we have time to go back to older emails, especially when new emails keep flowing in.

- *Reliability and accessibility.* As an Email Warrior, you end up being more consistently responsive. Before, you might have been sporadic in your response times. Now others can rely on a fairly timely response. This makes it much easier for other people to work with you.
- *Being more focused.* When your inbox is relatively clear, you minimize the associated distractions. This frees you up to focus on your top priorities and dig into bigger tasks. And when you focus on getting work done rather than being distracted by emails, you get more accomplished.

What comes next: After thirty days

After a month, you can shift your focus towards keeping up this habit indefinitely. However, I'm willing to bet that accomplishing this will be easier after thirty days. Once your embrace your Email Warrior status, there will be no turning back. Influencing other people to become Email Warriors just like you will also strengthen your resolve. Here are some suggestions to help you become an Email Warrior champion:

- Volunteer to lead a session for your team about how you become an Email Warrior.
- Tell people about how the One-Touch Principle has changed your life.

- Encourage people to set up a Master Plan—and use this to help clear their inbox.
- Advise others to streamline their email folders and clear out any reference emails clogging their inbox.
- Suggest your team adopt email protocols (and maybe even sign a team Email Charter).

As an Email Warrior, you are committing to a disciplined approach to managing your email. Take the Email Warrior Oath (see sidebar) to help remind yourself of the deliberate actions necessary to be an Email Warrior. Then go forth and continue to be awesome. You've got this!

The Email Warrior Oath

I will adopt the One-Touch Principle.

I will batch-process my email and stop multi-tasking.

I will sequentially process my email and be decisive.

I will move long-term tasks out of my inbox and onto my Master Plan.

I will get my inbox down to fewer than ten messages each day.

Acknowledgements

Writing this book presented me with amazing insight into how much people are willing to help. As a first-time author, I benefited from tremendous support from many people, including the following:

- All of our clients at Clear Concept Inc. who model excellent work habits, high-performance attitudes and clear inboxes. It is an honour to work with them.
- Frances, Geraldine, Marisa, Sarah, Susan and Teresa. I am humbled to have such an amazing team. Their input and collaboration has made this a much better product.
- Daphne Gray-Grant. I am immensely grateful to have her as my writing coach. She has taught me so much about writing and has helped me to develop a daily writing habit.
- Naomi Pauls, Duncan Watts-Grant and Island Blue Printing. This was a dynamic team who brought great expertise to this project with their thorough editing, creative design and superior service.
- Kathryn, Zeev and the amazing team at H2O Digital.
- Karen, who inspired a title I love: *The Email Warrior*.

- My friends and colleagues who encouraged me to write this book: Alyson, Dennis, Kareena, Laura, Lindsay, Michael and Nicole.
- Maricel, a tremendous supporter and good friend, to whom I am incredibly grateful.
- My father Charlie, late mother Lorraine, sister Laurie and Gomez in-laws, who have always supported me to pursue my dreams.
- Last on this list, but always first in my heart and mind: my family—Enrique, Christopher, Taylor, Michael and Daniel—who bring me joy every single day.

LOOKING FOR A SPEAKER?

Clear Concept Inc. is an international organization, training people to achieve their best work and their best life. Our interactive and engaging workshops help people become more productive and better leaders.

We work with busy people across industries. Recent clients include global law firms, financial institutions, consumer packaged goods, hospitals, and universities.

Author Ann Gomez is a sought-after expert on all topics related to productivity and leadership. Ann has appeared on national television, radio and print.

Featured programs include:

- Own Your Time
- The Leader Mindset
- Strategic Visioning
- Challenging Conversations
- Overcoming Procrastination
- Project Management Simplified
- Going Digital
- The Email Warrior

You can also access our comprehensive programs online. We offer live, interactive, webinars and on-demand training.

Implementation support

We offer customized individual or group implementation support. Topics include: setting up a priority management system, clearing email, establishing a priority-driven routine, office organization, delegation, project management, and other productivity or leadership goals.

Please visit www.clearconceptinc.ca for a full listing of our programs and services.

Contact us today to learn more about our engaging workshops and customized training.

info@clearconceptinc.ca
905.237.1651
www.clearconceptinc.ca

Connect with us on Social Media
Twitter: @ClearConceptInc
FaceBook: @clearconceptinc
LinkedIn: https://ca.linkedin.com/in/anngomez

Notes

Introduction
1 Merlin Mann, "43 Folders Series: Inbox Zero," 43 Folders, March 13, 2007, http://www.43folders.com/izero.

Chapter 1: Our Love Affair with Email
1 Ian Peter, "The History of Email," Net History (2004), http://www.nethistory.info/History%20of%20the%20Internet/email.html.
2 "Who Invented the Internet?" Computer Hope (2016), http://www.computerhope.com/issues/ch001016.htm.
3 "Official Biography: Raymond Tomlinson," Internet Hall of Fame (2016), http://www.internethalloffame.org/official-biography-raymond-tomlinson.
4 Quoted in Peter, "History of Email," para. 6.
5 William Grimes, "Raymond Tomlinson, Who Put the @ Sign in Email, Is Dead at 74," *The New York Times*, March 7, 2016, http://www.nytimes.com/2016/03/08/technology/raymond-tomlinson-email-obituary.html?_r=0.
6 Sasha Cavender, "Legends," *Forbes*, October 5, 1998, http://www.forbes.com/asap/1998/1005/126.html.

Chapter 2: Email Consumes Our Day
1 A 2011 study led by Fonality, a business communications company, found that workers at small and mid-size firms spend 50 percent of their workday on tasks such as email. Fonality & Webtorials, *2011 Report on UC and Cloud-Based Services for SMBs*. For a press release announcing research findings, see http://www.

fonality.com/blog/press-release/fonality-survey-finds-knowledge-workers-small-mid-size-firms-spend-half-workday. Similarly, a LexisNexis Workplace Productivity Survey based on 1,700 professionals in five countries found that "on average, workers report spending slightly more than half (51%) of their work day receiving and managing information, rather than actually using information to do their jobs." LexisNexis, "New Survey Reveals Extent, Impact of Information Overload on Workers" [Press release], October 20, 2010, http://www.lexisnexis.com/en-us/about-us/media/press-release.page?id=128751276114739. The most shocking study of all found that people spend a whopping 6.3 hours per day (or approximately 75 percent of their day) checking email. Patricia Reaney, "U.S. Workers Spend 6.3 Hours a Day Checking Email: Survey," *The Huffington Post*, August 26, 2015, http://m.huffpost.com/us/entry/check-work-email-hours-survey_us_55ddd168e4b0a40aa3ace672.

2   LexisNexis, "New Survey."

3   Chuck Klosterman, "My Zombie, Myself: Why Modern Life Feels Rather Undead," *The New York Times*, December 3, 2010, http://www.nytimes.com/2010/12/05/arts/television/05zombies.html?pagewanted=all.

4   Radicati Group, Inc., "Executive Summary," *Email Statistics Report, 2011–2015* (May 2011), http://www.radicati.com/wp/wp-content/uploads/2011/05/Email-Statistics-Report-2011-2015-Executive-Summary.pdf.

5   Statistic Brain Research Institute, "Attention Span Statistics" (2015; data sources: National Center for Biotechnology Information, U.S. National Library of Medicine, The Associated Press), http://www.statisticbrain.com/attention-span-statistics.

6   Anujeet Mojumdar, "Smartphone Users Check Their Phones an Average of 150 Times a Day," *Tech2*, May 30, 2013, http://tech.firstpost.com/news-analysis/smartphone-users-check-their-phones-an-average-of-150-times-a-day-86984.html.

7   Karen Renaud, Judith Ramsay, and Mario Hair, "'You've Got Email!'... Shall I Deal with It Now? Electronic Mail from the Recipient's Perspective," *International Journal of Human-Computer Interaction* 21, no. 3 (2015): 313–32, http://www.tandfonline.com/doi/abs/10.1207/s15327590ijhc2103_3 (available at http://interruptions.net/literature/Renaud-IJHCI06.pdf).

8   Thomas Jackson, Ray Dawson, and Darren Wilson, "Reducing the Effect of Email Interruptions on Employees," *International Journal of Information Management* 23, no. 1 (2003): 55–65 (available at http://jamesclear.com/wp-content/uploads/2015/02/email-multitasking-study.pdf).

9   Pew Internet Project, "Mobile Technology Fact Sheet" (Washington, DC: Pew Research Center, October 2014), http://www.pewinternet.org/fact-sheets/mobile-technology-fact-sheet. Professor Michelle Drouin at Indiana University–Purdue University found similar results: 89 percent of her undergraduate students experienced these phantom vibrations about every two weeks. As cited in Larry Rosen, "Phantom Pocket Vibration Syndrome," *Psychology Today*, May 7, 2013, https://www.psychologytoday.com/blog/rewired-the-psychology-technology/201305/phantom-pocket-vibration-syndrome.

10   Renaud and Ramsay's research was reported in "One in Three Workers Suffers from 'E-mail Stress,'" *The Telegraph*, August 13, 2007, http://www.telegraph.co.uk/news/uknews/1560148/One-in-three-workers-suffers-from-email-stress.html.

11   Reaney, "U.S. Workers." A 2010 AOL survey found that 62 percent of email users check work email over the weekend, and 19 percent check it five or more times in a weekend. The same AOL study also indicated that 50 to 78 percent of people check email while on vacation, with the highest number being mobile device users. AOL, "Email Addiction Results Are In," http://cdn.webmail.aol.com/survey/aol/en-us. Substantiating these data, an earlier study found that an alarming 83 percent of people check email while on vacation. AOL, "Think You Might Be Addicted to Email? You're Not Alone" [Press release], July 26, 2007, http://www.businesswire.com/news/home/20070726005167/en/Addicted-Email-Youre.

12   Sixty-five percent of U.S. smartphone users check their phones within 15 minutes of rising, and 64 percent check their phones within 15 minutes of going to bed. Heidi Cohen, "55 US Mobile Facts Every Marketer Needs for 2015" (December 8, 2014), http://heidicohen.com/2015-mobile-marketing.

13   Henry Blodget, "90% of 18-29 Year-Olds Sleep with Their Smartphones," *Business Insider*, November 21, 2012, http://www.businessinsider.com/90-of-18-29-year-olds-sleep-with-their-smartphones-2012-11.

14   Online Psychology Degree, "Getting in Bed with Gadgets" [Infographic], http://www.onlinepsychologydegree.net/2012/11/12/sleeping-with-gadgets.

15   David Boushy, "Most Canadians Admit to Distracted Driving: Poll," *Global News*, June 16, 2015, http://globalnews.ca/news/2056869/most-canadians-admit-to-distracted-driving-poll.

16   Centers for Disease Control and Prevention (CDC), "Distracted Driving" (March 7, 2016), http://www.cdc.gov/motorvehicle safety/distracted_driving.

17   Federal Communications Commission (FCC), "The Dangers of Texting While Driving" (November 4, 2015), https://www.fcc.gov/guides/texting-while-driving.

18   Ontario, Ministry of Transportation, "Distracted Driving" (n.d.), http://www.mto.gov.on.ca/english/safety/distracted-driving.shtml.

19   AOL, "Email Addiction Results."

20   S. Barley, D. Myerson, and S. Grodel, "E-mail as a Source and Symbol of Stress," *Organization Science* 22, no. 4 (2011): 887–906.

21   This study, led by Professor Tom Jackson of Loughborough University, looked at thirty government employees and examined their stress levels, based on saliva samples, over a 24-hour period. Eighty-three percent of participants became more stressed while using email, with stress levels peaking when their inboxes were the fullest. This number increased to 92 percent for those who were multi-tasking: speaking on the phone and using email at the same time. Nick Collins, "Email 'Raises Stress Levels,' " *The Tele-*

graph, June 4, 2013, http://www.telegraph.co.uk/news/science/science-news/10096907/Email-raises-stress-levels.html. In a 2012 study co-led by the University of California, Irvine and the United States Army, researchers found similar results. This study was based on having thirteen workers in a typical office setting discontinue email for five days. Their stress levels, measured using heart rate monitors, were much lower when they were not checking email regularly. When compared to their regular email use, they were less distracted when they discontinued email use. They demonstrated higher concentration levels during the non-email-use period, as evidenced by the fact that they switched between screens or programs approximately 18 times per hour. This was about half of their 37 times per hour during normal email use. Nick Bilton, "Taking E-mail Vacations Can Reduce Stress, Study Says," *The New York Times*, May 4, 2012, http://bits.blogs.nytimes.com/2012/05/04/taking-e-mail-vacations-can-reduce-stress-study-says/?_r=0.

22   Barley et al., "E-mail as a Source."

23   Collins, "Email 'Raises Stress Levels.' "

24   "One in Three Workers" (see note 10).

Chapter 3: Email Is Addictive

1   AOL, "Email Addiction Results Are In" (see chap. 2, note 11).

2   Tony Dokoupil, "Is the Internet Making Us Crazy? What the New Research Says," *Newsweek*, July 9, 2012, http://www.newsweek.com/internet-making-us-crazy-what-new-research-says-65593?piano_t=1.

3   Kelly McGonigal, *The Willpower Instinct: How Self-Control Works, Why It Matters, and What You Can Do to Get More of It* (New York: Avery, 2011), 114.

4   Cecilia Cheng and Angel Yee-lam Li, "Internet Addiction Prevalence and Quality of (Real) Life: A Meta-Analysis of 31 Nations Across Seven World Regions," *Cyberpsychology, Behavior, and Social Networking* 17, no. 12 (2014): 755–60, http://online.liebertpub.com/doi/abs/10.1089/cyber.2014.0317.

5   Chris Munch, "1.5 Years of Email Dopamine Addiction," *Munch-Web* (July 11, 2013), paras. 19–20, http://munchweb.com/addiction.

6   Statistic Brain Research Institute, "Attention Span Statistics" (2015), http://www.statisticbrain.com/attention-span-statistics.

7   Brian Wallace, "Facebook Psychology [Infographic]," *Social Media Today*, November 1, 2012, http://www.socialmediatoday.com/content/facebook-psychology-infographic.

8   A research team led by Hao Lei of the Chinese Academy of Sciences in Wuhan carried out brain scans of thirty-five men and women aged between 14 and 21. They found changes in the white matter of the brain in those classified as being web addicts, compared with non-addicts. Helen Briggs, "Web Addicts Have Brain Changes, Research Suggests," BBC News, January 12, 2012, http://www.bbc.com/news/health-16505521.

9   The *Diagnostic and Statistical Manual of Mental Disorders* (*DSM*) is published by the American Psychiatric Association and serves as an universal authority for psychiatric diagnosis.

10   Tony Schwartz, "Battling Your Online Addiction," *Harvard Business Review*, September 26, 2012, https://hbr.org/2012/09/the-addiction-that-plagues-us.html.

11   Research led by Hofmann revealed that relative to other addictive substances, the temptation to check social media was particularly hard to control. These researchers monitored the desires and willpower of 250 people in Germany. Participants were prompted to check in seven times per day over 14 hours for one week. They were asked to identify whether they were experiencing a desire to check social media in the previous 30 minutes. They were then asked to rate how strong the desire was and whether they chose to succumb to the desire or not. The temptation to check social media was found to be stronger than the temptation associated with nicotine, alcohol and sex. W. Hofmann, R.F. Bau-

meister, G. Förster, and K.D. Vohs, "Everyday Temptations: An Experience Sampling Study of Desire, Conflict, and Self-Control," *Journal of Personality and Society Psychology* 102, no. 6 (2012): 1318–35, http://www.ncbi.nlm.nih.gov/pubmed/22149456. See also James Meikle, "Twitter Is Harder to Resist Than Cigarettes and Alcohol, Study Finds," *The Guardian*, February 3, 2012, http://www.guardian.co.uk/technology/2012/feb/03/twitter-resist-cigarettes-alcohol-study?newsfeed=true.

12   Belle Beth Cooper, "Why Getting New Things Makes Us Feel So Good: Novelty and the Brain," *Buffer*, May 16, 2013, https://blog.bufferapp.com/novelty-and-the-brain-how-to-learn-more-and-improve-your-memory.

13   Susan Weinschenk, "100 Things You Should Know About People: #8—Dopamine Makes You Addicted to Seeking Information," *The Team W Blog*, November 7, 2009, http://www.blog.theteamw.com/2009/11/07/100-things-you-should-know-about-people-8-dopamine-makes-us-addicted-to-seeking-information.

14   Daniel Snyder, "Intermittent Reinforcement—Are You Addicted to Email and Smartphones?" Knoji.com (September 1, 2010), https://knoji.com/intermittent-reinforcement-are-you-addicted-to-email-and-smartphones.

Chapter 4: Flawed Strategy 1: Multi-tasking

1   Brendon Burchard, "5 50-Minute Habits Get You 30% More Productive (and Energized)" [Video],http://2.highperformanceacademy.com/5x50video?autoplay=1&utm_source=brendoncom&utm_medium=optin&utm_campaign=hpa-popup.

2   This exercise was inspired by Dave Crenshaw, who describes a similar exercise in his compelling book *The Myth of Multitasking: How "Doing It All" Gets Nothing Done* (San Francisco: Jossey-Bass, 2008).

3   Shamsi T. Iqbal and Eric Horvitz, "Disruption and Recovery of

Computing Tasks: Field Study, Analysis, and Directions" (paper presented at the SIGCHI conference on Human Factors in Computing Systems, San Francisco, CA, April 30–May 3, 2007), http://research.microsoft.com/en-us/um/people/horvitz/chi_2007_iqbal_horvitz.pdf; see also Rachel Emma Silverman, "Workplace Distractions: Here's Why You Won't Finish This Article," *The Wall Street Journal*, December 11, 2012.

4   Thomas Jackson, Ray Dawson, and Darren Wilson, "The Cost of Email Interruption" (n.d.), http://interruptions.net/literature/Jackson-JOSIT-01.pdf.

5   Gloria Mark, Daniela Gudith, and Ulrich Klocke, "The Cost of Interrupted Work: More Speed and Stress" (n.d.), https://www.ics.uci.edu/~gmark/chi08-mark.pdf.

6   Ibid.

7   Gloria Mark, interview, "Too Many Interruptions at Work?" *Gallup Business Journal*, June 8, 2006, http://www.gallup.com/businessjournal/23146/too-many-interruptions-work.aspx.

8   Renaud et al., "'You've Got Email'" (see chap. 2, note 7).

Chapter 5: Flawed Strategy 2: Triaging

1   Admittedly, some emails take more time and some take less time, but 30 seconds to read an email seems to work as an average. Feel free to adjust these calculations to reflect your experience.

Chapter 8: Strategy 1: Dedicate Time

1   Jim Loehr and Tony Schwartz, *The Power of Full Engagement: Managing Energy, Not Time, Is the Key to High Performance and Personal Renewal* (New York: Free Press, 2005), 31.

Chapter 9: Strategy 2: Do It

1   You may also choose to unsubscribe from messages you no lon-

ger wish to receive. Bulk emails (such as newsletters) should have an "Unsubscribe" or "Manage my subscription" link at the bottom. Click on this and follow the directions to permanently remove yourself from the list.

2   Malcolm Gladwell, *Blink: The Power of Thinking without Thinking* (New York: Back Bay Books, 2006).

3   Most email systems allow you to set an auto-delete schedule, whereby you decide how long emails sit in your trash folder. For example, if your setting is to clear out any emails from your deleted folder that are older than three months, then you can always re-trieve the most recent emails. It helps to know when emails in your deleted folder get automatically purged (check your own program settings). For example, Gmail's default is to delete email from its trash bin after 30 days.

Chapter 10: Strategy 3: Defer It

1   This quote has been adopted by many different people. It orig-inates from Simon Fulleringer, Asset & Configuration Management Process Manager at McGill University. Find his LinkedIn profile at http://ca.linkedin.com/pub/simon-fulleringer/27/218/523.

2   George A. Miller, "The Magical Number Seven, Plus or Minus Two: Some Limits on Our Capacity for Processing Information," *Psychological Review* 63 (1956): 81–97, http://psychclassics.yorku.ca/Miller.

3   "The Magical Number Seven Plus or Minus Two," *Coding Horror* [Blog] (August 14, 2006), https://blog.codinghorror.com/the-magical-number-seven-plus-or-minus-two.

4   Nelson Cowan, "The Magical Number 4 in Short-Term Memory: A Reconsideration of Mental Storage Capacity," *Behavioural and Brain Sciences* 24, no. 1 (February 2001): 87–114, http://journals.cambridge.org/action/displayAbstract?fromPage=online&aid=84441; Josh Hill, "The Limits of Memory: We Can Only Remember Four

Things at a Time," *The Digital Galaxy* (April 29, 2008), http://www.dailygalaxy.com/my_weblog/2008/04/the-limits-of-m.html.

5   "Age Associated Memory Impairment," *The Human Memory* [Website] (2010), http://www.human-memory.net/disorders_age.html.

6   J.J. Kim, E.Y. Song, and T.A. Kosten, "Stress Effects in the Hippocampus: Synaptic Plasticity and Memory," *Stress* 9, no. 1 (March 2006): 9–11, http://www.ncbi.nlm.nih.gov/pubmed/16753928.

7   Carmen Sandi, "Memory Impairments Associated with Stress and Aging," chap. 12 in *Neural Plasticity and Memory: From Genes to Brain Imaging*, ed. Federico Bermúdez-Rattoni (Boca Raton, FL: CRC Press / Taylor & Francis, 2007), http://www.ncbi.nlm.nih.gov/books/NBK3914.

8   This appears to be related to being thoroughly familiar with the material. For example, chess masters are able to remember chessboard configurations much better than novices. However, when the chess pieces are moved into random formations (i.e., not associated with actual configurations the chess masters may have encountered before), their recall drops to similar levels as novice chess players.

Chapter 11: Step 1: Build Your Master Plan

1   Stephen R. Covey, "Habit 7: Sharpen the Saw," from *The 7 Habits of Highly Effective People: Powerful Lessons in Personal Change* (New York: Free Press, 1989), https://www.stephencovey.com/7habits/7habits-habit7.php.

2   More than a century before Covey's time, a sermon titled "The Dull Axe" was published in a periodical of the Presbyterian Church of the U.S.A. with reference to a woodcutter "sharpening his axe." "Sermons for the Times: No. 2: The Dull Axe" (from the *New York Evangelist*), *The Home and Foreign Record of the Presbyterian*

Church in the United States of America, vol. 7, no. 1 (Philadelphia, PA: Publication House, 1856), p. 8, col. 1, http://quoteinvestigator.com/2014/03/29/sharp-axe/#return-note-8542-2.
3   When you write something down with a pen on paper, you are stimulating a collection of cells in the base of your brain known as the reticular activating system (RAS). Your RAS is the filter for all of the information your brain needs to process. The physical act of writing triggers your brain to pay close attention. "How Does Writing Affect Your Brain?" *NeuroRelay* [Blog] (August 7, 2013), http://neurorelay.com/2013/08/07/how-does-writing-affect-your-brain. Interestingly, writing notes seems to have a better impact on memory than does typing notes. Studies show students who took notes on laptops performed worse on conceptual questions than students who took notes longhand. This was explained by the laptop note takers' tendency to transcribe lectures verbatim rather than processing information and reframing it in their own words. Pam A. Mueller and Daniel M. Oppenheimer, "The Pen Is Mightier Than the Keyboard: Advantages of Longhand Over Laptop Note Taking," *Psychological Science* 25, no. 6 (June 2014): 1159–68, http://pss.sagepub.com/content/25/6/1159.

Chapter 12: Step 2: Streamline Your Storage System
1   Thomas Jackson, "Email Stress," *Dr Jackson's Research* (n.d.), http://www.profjackson.com/email_stress.html.
2   Caution: the term "archiving" can also be used to refer to older emails being relocated from your email folders into a central archive. When I use the term "archiving," I refer to moving emails out of your inbox into one folder (or label).

Chapter 13: Step 3: Clear Your Inbox
1   Note: While I agree that ten is an arbitrary goal, I also fundamentally believe that a benchmark close to this will help you to keep your inbox relatively clear.

Index

accessibility, 7, 76, 79, 165
addiction, 31–40, 174n8
alerts, 37, 45, 52, 76–77, 78, 81
Allen, David, 110
applications, task-tracking, 124
archiving, 135–36, 137, 149, 179n2
attention spans, 33. *See also*
    focused work

backlog, 7, 55–56, 88, 150–51, 163
batch-processing, 10, 70, 76, 139,
    149, 151
brain, 32, 33, 35–37, 174n8.
    See also memory
Burchard, Brendon, 43–44, 45

capacity, 109. *See also*
    overcommitment
Clear Concept Inc., 4, 46, 152, 184
clearing your inbox, 147–57, 162–64.
    See also deleting email
Cloutier, Michael, 3, 93
collaboration, 16, 29, 109, 129
communication, 16, 19, 72, 89, 97
Covey, Stephen R., 116

deadlines, 56, 109, 120–21, 125, 163
decision-making, 6, 89, 92, 95, 164
deleting email, 95, 99–103, 134,
    177n3. *See also* clearing your inbox
distracted driving, 26
distractions, 49, 57, 62, 151, 165,
    173n21
DMS (document management
    system), 136

email
  about, 15–22, 27–29
  addiction, 31–40
  checking, 23–26, 171n11, 172n12
  responses, 39, 72, 97, 160–62
  statistics, 169–70n1
  as a tool, 4, 49, 72–73
  urgent, 73–74, 80, 86, 93–94, 96
  See also inbox; One-Touch Principle
email management
  exemplars, 2, 3, 10, 88, 152
  flawed strategies, 27, 43–62
  processing frequency, 74–76, 79
  3D Approach, 65–112, 154–56, 160
  what to delete / keep, 100–103
email storage system, 59, 127, 133–45,
    149
email systems
  auto functions, 101, 102, 139, 177n3
  folders, 135–36, 142, 143
  task management, 124–25
Email Warrior
  action plan, 131–32, 145, 157
  benefits, 5–7, 164–65
  goals, 56, 85, 133, 160, 179n1
  strategies, 65–112, 154–56, 160
  30-Day Challenge, 159–65
emotions, 3, 61, 97, 107, 156
etiquette, 73, 81, 97
expectations, 20, 72, 75–76, 79–80,
    109, 115

filing system, 59, 127, 133–45, 149
focus, improved, 7, 121, 165
focused work, 45–46, 69, 70, 74–75,
    76, 108

folders, 59, 127, 135–45
forgetting, 32, 60, 81–82, 107, 155.
   See also memory
Fulleringer, Simon, 108, 177n1

Gladwell, Malcolm, 89
goals, 34, 56, 85, 121, 133, 160, 179n1
Gray-Grant, Daphne, 10

Hill, Napoleon, 120
hoarding email, 57–62
Hofmann, Wilhelm, 34, 174–75n11

IAD (Internet Addiction Disorder), 33
inbox
  clearing your, 147–57
  downsides of clogged, 6, 60–61
  functions, 58–59, 62, 65, 127
  See also One-Touch Principle
"Inbox Zero," 4, 156
instant gratification, 34, 36–37
Internet, 17, 20, 32–33, 174n8
interruptions, 48–49, 71, 81. *See also*
  sleep

Jackson, Thomas, 47, 134, 172–73n21

Kleinrock, Leonard, 17

Mann, Merlin, 4
Mark, Gloria, 47, 48
Master Plan, 115–32, 148–49, 155
  features, 116–22, 123
  formats, 123–26, 127–28
  functions, 106–9, 112, 115
McGonigal, Kelly, 32
memory, 59, 110–12, 127, 178n8,
  179n3. *See also* forgetting

millennials, 25, 26, 174n8
Miller's Law, 110
multi-tasking, 28, 45–48, 70, 172n21,
  175n2
Munch, Chris, 32

One-Touch Principle, 84–103
  and clearing inbox, 149, 154
  tips on applying, 91–99
overcommitment, 59, 109, 118,
  162–63

Parkinson's Law, 121
personal time, 25–26, 45, 98
Postel, Jon, 18
prioritizing, 6, 53, 61, 108, 160–62.
  See also Master Plan
procrastination, 34, 40, 92, 121
productivity, 5, 96, 74, 170n1
  clear vs. clogged inbox, 61, 100
  email and, 15, 19, 49, 71, 160
  tool (*see* Master Plan)
  training, 4, 46, 152, 175n2, 184

quality of life, 32. *See also* personal
  time
quality work, 7, 47, 79

Ramsay, Judith, 24
redundant reading, 53–55, 71, 84, 87,
  98, 101
reference material, 44, 58, 99, 101,
  134
Renaud, Karen, 24, 48, 49
responsiveness, 6–7, 39–40, 165
reward system, 36–37, 38, 80, 92, 150
Rockefeller, John D., 7

Schwartz, Tony, 34
search functionality, 136, 137, 141
self-regulation, 34, 48, 49
sequential processing, 91–93, 153–54
"sharpening the saw," 116, 117, 178n2
sleep, 25–26, 78, 98, 163
smartphones
 checking, 26, 37, 172n12
 email and, 45, 76, 77, 78, 96, 171n11
 "phantom vibrations," 24, 171n9
social media, 31–32, 174n11
software, 123–25. *See also* email
 systems
stress, 27–29, 47–48, 111, 134,
 172–73n21

task management. *See* Master Plan
tasks, 58, 86–87, 119, 129, 155–56,
 161. *See also* prioritizing; to-do lists
teams, 1–2, 51–52, 97, 136
technology, as addictive, 32
3D Approach, 65–112, 154–56, 160
 acting on email, 83–103
 dedicating time, 69–82
 deferring email, 105–12
time management, 5, 11
 acting on email, 69–82
 clearing inbox, 148
 filing email, 100
 low-priority emails, 161–62
 statistics, 169–70n1
 wasted time, 6, 47, 53–55, 61, 95, 96
 See also One-Touch Principle;
  personal time

to-do folders, 127
to-do lists
 effective (*see* Master Plan)
 ineffective, 44, 58, 62, 110, 127
 short-term, 130, 155
Tomlinson, Ray, 18–19
triaging strategy, 52–56

unsubscribing, 176–77n1
urgent emails, 73–74, 80, 86, 93–94,
 96

vacation, 88, 171n11

willpower, 32, 76, 174n11
writing things down, 118, 125–26,
 179n3

About the Author

Ann Gomez founded Clear Concept Inc. in 2004 with the vision to help busy people pursue fulfilling work and extraordinary lives. Since then, Ann and her team have developed several popular productivity and high-performance team training programs. One of their most popular programs is The Email Warrior. Through it they have helped thousands of people to clear their inboxes and find more time in their days. Ann and her husband live north of Toronto with their four active children.

BONUS TRAINING

Ready to clear your inbox and keep it that way?

Watch The Email Warrior companion
video series at no extra charge.

You'll get in-depth training about how
The Email Warrior system works.

Get your videos at:

https://clearconceptinc.ca/bonusvideos/

Made in the USA
Middletown, DE
05 January 2019